Healthy Egg and Potato Nests

2 medium potatoes, peeled and chopped

1½ cups rainbow chard (silverbeet or spinach would be fine too), chopped

4 eggs

½ cup (60g) cheese, grated

Bring potatoes to the boil in a medium saucepan of salted water. Reduce the heat and cook on a simmer for 12 minutes until tender. Drain and mash. (Add butter or cream to your preference.) Set aside to cool slightly.

When cool, add potato to a piping bag and carefully squirt into the bottom and around the edges of the pie maker holes, making sure to leave enough space for the filling.

Gently press equal quantities of the chard into the centre of each hole.

Break egg into a cup and gently transfer to a pie hole. Repeat with the remaining eggs.

Sprinkle equal quantities of the cheese over each egg.

Close the lid and cook for 6 minutes.

Let the pies rest for a minute and then remove with a plastic or wooden spatula.

MAKES 4 SMALL PIES

Tip:
• *This is a great recipe for using up leftover mash.*

Feta and Chive Egg Muffins

2 eggs, beaten

1½ tbsps milk

¼ cup (60g) hard feta, crumbled

1 tbsp chives, chopped

¼ cup (20g) self-raising flour

¼ cup (30g) tasty cheese, grated

Whisk the egg and milk together in large jug. Add in the feta, chives, flour and tasty cheese and gently stir to combine.

Pour the mixture into the holes of the pie maker and close the lid.

Cook for 8 minutes or until golden.

MAKES 4

Corn Fritters

1¾ cups (300g) corn kernels (fresh or frozen)

¾ cup (100g) plain flour

½ tsp baking powder

⅓ cup (50g) cornflour

1 cup (125g) tasty cheese, grated

2 spring onions, finely chopped

Pinch of salt and pepper

1 egg

½ cup (125ml) milk (as needed)

Fry the corn in a large frying pan over a high heat for 3 minutes, or until slightly charred. Set aside.

Place the remaining ingredients apart from the milk in a large mixing bowl and stir well to combine. Add the corn and stir again to mix it through.

Slowly add the milk and keep stirring until a thick batter forms. You may not need to add all the milk.

Using lightly floured hands, shape the mixture into patties. Gently place the patties into the holes of the pie maker.

Cook for 5 minutes or until golden, turning once halfway through cooking.

Let the fritters rest for a minute and then remove with a plastic or wooden spatula.

MAKES 12

Epic Breakfast Muffins

4 eggs

¼ cup (60ml) milk

⅓ cup (40g) self-raising flour

125g thick-cut ham

2 sprigs of basil, leaves picked and chopped

2 tomatoes, chopped

½ yellow capsicum, deseeded and chopped

¾ cup (90g) tasty cheese

Lightly whisk the eggs and milk together in large jug. Add the flour and stir well. Add in the remaining ingredients and gently stir to combine.

Pour the mixture into the holes of the pie maker and close the lid.

Cook for 8 minutes or until golden.

Let the muffins rest for a minute and then remove with a plastic or wooden spatula.

MAKES 8

Sweet Potato Hash Browns

250g sweet potato, grated

2 eggs

1 small onion, grated

½ cup (60g) tasty cheese, grated

Pinch of salt and pepper

Put the grated sweet potato in a clean tea towel and squeeze out the excess liquid.

Place potato in a large mixing bowl and add the other ingredients. Stir well to combine.

Spoon the mixture into the holes in equal measure.

Close the lid and cook for around 15 minutes, flipping halfway through cooking.

MAKES 4

Tip:

• You can make this recipe with regular potatoes too if preferred.

Mushroom and Oregano Frittata

Olive oil, for frying

150g mixed mushrooms

½ cup (60g) Parmesan cheese, grated

1½ tsps fresh oregano, chopped (or 1 tsp dried oregano)

¼ tsp black pepper

⅛ tsp salt

5 eggs, lightly beaten

¼ cup (60ml) milk

Heat oil in a large frying pan over medium-high heat. Add mushrooms to pan and saute for a few minutes until tender.

Place mushrooms in a medium-sized mixing bowl and add the cheese, oregano, pepper, salt, eggs and milk and stir until well combined.

Pour into the holes of the pie maker and close the lid.

Cook for 6 minutes.

Let the frittatas rest for a minute and then remove with a plastic or wooden spatula.

MAKES 4

Tip:

• Supermarkets sell small packs of exotic mushrooms which would be great to use in this recipe.

Pikelets

1 egg

¼ cup (60ml) milk

1 cup (125g) self-raising flour

¼ tsp bicarbonate of soda

¼ cup (55g) caster sugar

30g butter, melted

Fresh berries and icing sugar, to serve

Whisk together the egg and milk.

Sift flour and bicarb together into a medium bowl and then stir in the sugar. Using a wooden spoon, make a well in centre. Gradually stir in the egg and milk until the mixture is pourable. If time allows, set aside for 10 minutes so the mixture can rest.

Pour the batter into each hole of the heated pie maker in equal measure.

Close and cook for 6 minutes, flipping halfway through cooking.

Let the pikelets rest for a minute and then remove with a plastic or wooden spatula.

SERVES 4

Hack it!

• Use a store-bought pancake shake mix such as Green's Original Pancake Shake to make this recipe even quicker and easier.

Almond Pancakes

2 cups (200g) almond flour

1 cup (270ml) coconut milk

¼ cup (90g) honey

4 eggs

15g butter

1 tsp baking powder

Pinch of salt

1 tsp vanilla

Whisk together all the ingredients in a large mixing bowl until a smooth batter forms.

Pour the batter into each hole in equal measure.

Close and cook for 6 minutes, flipping halfway through cooking.

Let the pancakes rest for a minute and then remove with a plastic or wooden spatula.

SERVES 4

French Toast with Berries

Splash of milk

1 egg, lightly whisked

Pinch of cinnamon (optional)

4 slices thick white bread

1½ cups (250g) fresh berries

¼ cup (80g) maple syrup

In a bowl, combine milk, egg and cinnamon.

Use an egg ring to cut circles out of the bread. Dip the bread circles into the egg mixture. Turn over to coat the other side.

Transfer to the pie maker and cook for approximately 5 minutes until golden, flipping halfway through cooking. Check after 2 minutes to ensure the French toast does not get overdone.

Serve hot with butter, maple syrup and fresh berries.

MAKES 4

Simple Blueberry Muffins

60g butter

1 egg

1 cup (250ml) buttermilk

2 cups (250g) self-raising flour

¾ cup (120g) brown sugar

1¼ cups (125g) blueberries

Heat the butter in a small pan over medium heat (or use a microwave) until just melted and then set aside.

Beat the egg in a mixing bowl and then stir in the buttermilk and melted butter.

Sift the flour into a second mixing bowl. Add the sugar and stir to combine.

Pour the wet ingredients into the dry ingredients and gently stir to bring the batter together. Don't over-mix it. It should still have some lumps.

Fold in the blueberries.

Pour the mixture into the holes of the pie maker and close the lid.

Close the lid and cook for 6 minutes.

Let the muffins rest for a minute and then remove with a plastic or wooden spatula.

MAKES 8

Hack it!

• *Use a muffin mix such as Betty Crocker Blueberry Muffin Mix to make this recipe even quicker and easier.*

Gluten-Free Quinoa Muffins

1¾ cups (190g) quinoa flour

2 tsps baking powder

Pinch of salt

1 egg, lightly beaten

⅓ cup (80ml) soy milk

¼ cup (60ml) vegetable or canola oil

½ tsp lemon zest

2 tsps agave syrup

Sift together the flour, baking powder and salt in a large mixing bowl and make a well in the centre.

Whisk together the egg, milk, oil, zest and agave.

Pour the wet ingredients into the well and mix until a thick batter forms.

Pour even amounts of the batter into each pie maker hole, filling each hole three-quarters full.

Close the lid and cook for 10 minutes until golden brown on top or until a skewer inserted into the middle of one comes out clean.

MAKES 12

Gluten-Free Strawberry Muffins

2½ cups (220g) oat flour

2 tsps mixed spice

1 cup (160g) light brown sugar

1 cup (250ml) soy or cow's milk

½ cup (125ml) vegetable or canola oil

1 large egg, lightly beaten

1 cup (210g) strawberries, chopped (or use frozen)

Whisk together the dry ingredients in a large mixing bowl and make a well in the centre.

Beat together the milk, oil and egg.

Pour the wet ingredients into the well and mix until a thick batter forms.

Fold in the strawberries.

Pour even amounts of the batter into each pie maker hole, filling each hole three-quarters full.

Close the lid and cook for 10 minutes until golden brown on top or until a skewer inserted into the middle of one comes out clean.

MAKES 12

Tip:

• *If muffins are not cooked through but they are brown enough for you, then you can finish by popping in the microwave for a minute or two.*

Blueberry Bran Muffins

2 cups (190g) oat bran

1 cup (125g) wholemeal flour

½ tsp bicarbonate of soda

1 tsp mixed spice

2 large bananas, mashed

⅔ cup (160ml) milk

¼ cup (80g) maple syrup

1 large egg, lightly beaten

25g butter, melted

2 cups (210g) blueberries (fresh or frozen)

Mix together the dry ingredients in a large mixing bowl and make a well in the centre.

Beat together the bananas, milk, maple syrup, egg and butter.

Pour the wet ingredients into the well and mix until a thick batter forms.

Fold in the blueberries.

Pour even amounts of the batter into each pie maker hole, filling each hole three-quarters full.

Close the lid and cook for 12 minutes until golden brown on top or until a skewer inserted into the middle of one comes out clean.

MAKES 12

Coconut Jam Drops

1 x 395g can sweetened condensed milk

125g butter, chopped

½ cup (125ml) milk

1 cup (125g) self-raising flour

1 cup (90g) desiccated coconut

1 egg

¾ cup (245g) raspberry jam

Heat the condensed milk, butter and milk in the microwave on high for 2 minutes or until the butter has melted. Stir the mixture to combine and set aside to cool slightly.

Stir together the flour and coconut in a large bowl. Add the condensed milk mixture and the egg and whisk together to form a lumpy batter.

Scoop a tablespoon of batter into each hole to cover the base. Spoon in the raspberry jam and then fill the holes with batter.

Close the lid and cook for 8 minutes until golden.

Let the jam drops rest for a minute and then remove with a plastic or wooden spatula.

MAKES 10

Tip:
• Use this batter mixture for different flavours such as apple or choc chip. Just swap the raspberry jam for another centre of your choice.

Apricot Bran Muffins

1½ cups (140g) oat bran

1 cup (90g) oat flour

2 tsps baking powder

1 tsp cinnamon

Pinch of salt

⅓ cup (80ml) Greek yoghurt

1 large egg, lightly beaten

½ cup (155g) maple syrup

1 tbsp butter, melted

6 apricots, halved

Stir together the dry ingredients in a large mixing bowl and make a well in the centre.

Beat together the yoghurt, egg, maple syrup and butter.

Pour the wet ingredients into the well and mix until a thick batter forms.

Pour even amounts of the batter into each pie maker hole, filling each hole three-quarters full.

Press an apricot half, cut-side up, into the top of each muffin.

Close the lid and cook for 15 minutes until golden brown on top and cooked through.

MAKES 12

Apple and Oat Muffins with Orange Syrup

1 x 600g packet vanilla mud cake mix

1 cup (90g) quick oats

1 tsp cinnamon

½ cup (60g) walnuts

2 eggs

¼ cup (60ml) olive oil

¾ cup (185ml) coconut cream

2½ cups (400g) stewed apples

1 cup (220g) sugar

½ cup (125ml) water

¾ cup (185ml) orange juice, freshly squeezed

1 tbsp cornflour

2 tbsps butter

¼ cup (30g) flaked almonds

Place the cake mix, oats, cinnamon and walnuts into a mixing bowl and stir to combine.

Whisk together the eggs, olive oil and coconut cream in a separate bowl. Gently fold in the apples.

Pour the wet ingredients into the dry ingredients and gently stir to bring the batter together. Don't over-mix it. It should still have some lumps.

Pour the mixture into the holes of the pie maker and close the lid. You will need to make several batches.

Cook for 8 minutes or until golden.

To make the syrup, place the sugar and water in a small saucepan and bring to a boil, stirring continuously. In a small bowl, combine the orange juice and cornflour to create a slurry. Pour the slurry into the saucepan and simmer gently, stirring, until thickened. When thick add the butter and stir until glossy.

Pour the syrup over the muffins to serve and decorate with flaked almonds.

MAKES 18

Healthy Breakfast Muffins

1½ cups (150g) almond flour

¼ cup (40g) brown sugar

2 tbsps raw cacao powder

1 banana, mashed

50g butter, melted

1 egg, lightly beaten

¼ tsp vanilla extract

⅛ cup milk

Whisk together the dry ingredients in a large mixing bowl and make a well in the centre.

Beat together the banana, butter, egg, vanilla and milk.

Pour the wet ingredients into the well and mix until a thick batter forms.

Pour even amounts of the batter into each pie maker hole, filling each hole three-quarters full.

Close the lid and cook for 10 minutes until cooked through and a skewer inserted into the middle of one comes out clean.

MAKES 8

Hack it!

• To make it so easy (if a bit less healthy) use a packet of chocolate muffin mix instead. Cook for 10 minutes.

Quick and Easy Banana Muffins

2 cups (250g) self-raising flour

⅔ cup (100g) light brown sugar

1 tsp baking powder

½ tsp bicarbonate of soda

1 tsp mixed spice (optional)

3 medium bananas; 2 mashed, 1 cut into 12 slices

½ cup (125ml) milk

⅓ cup (80ml) butter, melted

2 medium eggs, lightly beaten

½ tsp vanilla extract

Mix together the dry ingredients in a large mixing bowl and make a well in the centre.

Beat together the mashed bananas, milk, butter, eggs and vanilla.

Pour the wet ingredients into the well and mix until a thick batter forms.

Pour even amounts of the batter into each pie maker hole, filling each hole three-quarters full.

Press a slice of banana into the top of each muffin.

Close the lid and cook for 12 minutes until golden brown on top or until a skewer inserted into the middle of one comes out clean.

Serve warm or cold.

MAKES 12

Hack it!

• To make this even easier, you could use a butter cake packet mix. Combine the mix with a tablespoon of oil and ¼ cup (40g) chia or flax seeds, two tablespoons of honey and three mashed bananas. Cook in the pie maker for 10 minutes.

Snacks

Camembert and Quince Fondue Pie

1 egg

1 tbsp milk

1 sheet frozen puff pastry

2 tbsps quince paste

1 x 200g camembert round

Whisk together the egg and milk in a bowl to create an egg wash.

Place the sheet of puff pastry on a lightly floured work surface.

Place the round of camembert in the middle. Spoon the quince paste on top and smooth over with a knife. Fold the pastry over to cover. Place the parcel, seam-side down, in the hole of a family pie maker. Brush the egg wash over the pastry.

Close the lid and cook for 15 minutes.

Let the pie rest for a minute and then remove with a plastic or wooden spatula.

MAKES 1 MEDIUM PIE

Tip:

• To make four individual pies, cut the pastry sheet into quarters and place them into the holes of the pie maker with the edges hanging over. Cut the cheese into pieces that will fit in the holes and cover with quince paste. Wrap the pastry over the top so the cheese is sealed inside. Cook for 10 minutes until golden.

Cheese and Tomato Bites

2 eggs, beaten

1 cup (250ml) thickened cream

½ cup (15g) basil, chopped

¼ tsp pepper

1½ sheets puff pastry

12 cherry tomatoes, halved

Basil leaves, to garnish

Combine the egg, cream, basil leaves and pepper in a mixing bowl.

Cut six circles from the pastry and place them into your pie maker.

Pour mixture into the pastry bases and arrange the tomatoes on top.

Close the lid and cook for 10 minutes.

Remove and set aside to cool. Garnish with basil leaves to serve.

MAKES 6

Hot Dog and Ketchup Puffs

2 sheets puff pastry

1⅔ cups (200g) tasty cheese, grated

¼ cup (60ml) tomato sauce

8 cocktail franks, cut in half

Cut each sheet of pastry into 4 squares. Press the pastry squares into the holes of the pie maker.

For each pie hole, spoon in the tomato ketchup then sprinkle the cheese over the top. Stick a cocktail frank half into each.

Close the lid and cook for 4-5 minutes or until cheese has melted and pastry is cooked.

MAKES 8

Salmon and Spinach Quiche

1 batch of shortcrust pastry (store-bought or see recipe page 14)

200g frozen spinach

½ tbsp butter, melted

3 small eggs, lightly beaten

1¼ cups (300ml) creme fraiche (or sour cream)

⅓ cup (100ml) cream

Salt and pepper

200g fresh salmon, filleted and roughly chopped

Roll out the pastry to the desired thickness on a lightly floured workbench.

Cut the pastry into a round to fit your family pie maker, remembering it needs to extend up the sides too.

Beat together the spinach, butter, eggs, creme fraiche, cream and a pinch each of salt and pepper.

Gently fold through the salmon.

Press the pastry into the family pie maker and pour in the filling to just under the edges of the pastry.

Close the lid and cook for 20 minutes. Turn off the pie maker and let the filling set for 5 minutes before removing from the pie maker.

MAKES 1 FAMILY PIE

Stuffed Mushrooms

1 tbsp olive oil

3 rashers thin cut bacon, trimmed

½ small onion, chopped

1 clove garlic, minced

¼ cup (30g) breadcrumbs

35g soft goat's cheese, crumbled

Salt and pepper

6 brown mushrooms

¼ cup (30g) mozzarella cheese, grated

Heat half the oil in large frying pan over a medium-high heat. Cook the bacon until crispy and set aside. Add remaining oil and cook the onion for a few minutes until soft. Add garlic and fry for a further 30 seconds. Remove from the heat.

Add breadcrumbs to the mixture and stir to combine. Add goat's cheese, salt and pepper and bacon and toss gently.

Place a mushroom into each hole of the pie maker. Spoon the breadcrumb mixture into each mushroom. Sprinkle with mozzarella.

Close the lid and cook for 6 minutes.

MAKES 6

Lasagne Cups

30g butter

½ cup (60g) plain flour

2 cups (500ml) milk

1 cup (125g) tasty cheese, grated

1 tbsp olive oil

500g beef mince

1½ cups (350g) passata

12 fresh lasagne sheets

To make the cheese sauce first melt the butter in a small saucepan over medium heat. Add the flour and stir well. Slowly and gradually add the milk, stirring constantly to avoid lumps. Add half of the cheese and stir until just melted. Remove from the heat and set aside.

Heat the olive oil in a large frying pan. When hot add the mince and fry for 3-4 minutes until browned.

Stir in the passata and cheese sauce and remove from the heat.

Cut circles slightly larger than your pie maker holes from the lasagne sheets. Place a lasagne circle in the base of each hole, then spoon in some of the filling mixture until about half full. Place another piece of lasagne over the top and again add a spoonful or two of filling until about three-quarters full. Sprinkle cheese over the top.

Close the lid and cook for 10 minutes.

Makes 6

Tip:

• You can use the easy bolognaise recipe on page 103 for this or if you have leftover bolognaise this is a great way to use it up.

Spaghetti Pie

180g spaghetti, broken in half

1½ tbsps butter

Oil, for frying

1 small onion, chopped

2 small cloves garlic, minced

8 rashers bacon, chopped

6 medium eggs, lightly beaten

⅓ cup (80ml) milk

¼ cup (25g) Parmesan cheese, grated

Salt and pepper

Cook the spaghetti according to packet directions until al dente. Drain, toss with ½ tablespoon of the butter and set aside.

Heat a splash of oil a medium frying pan over medium heat and fry the onion, garlic and bacon for 5 minutes. Remove to a large mixing bowl.

Add the remaining butter, eggs and milk and mix everything together thoroughly. Add the spaghetti and mix through with the cheese and a couple of grinds of salt and pepper.

Place the mixture in the base of a family pie maker (or place half cups of mixture in individual pie maker holes).

Close the lid and cook for 15 minutes until golden brown on top, slightly crispy on the edges and cooked through.

MAKES 1 FAMILY PIE OR 8 SMALL PIES

Macaroni Cheese Pies

2 cups (200g) macaroni or elbow pasta

1½ tbsps butter

1 large egg, lightly beaten

1 cup (250ml) milk

3 cups (375g) mixed cheese (such as mozzarella, Parmesan, tasty)

1 tsp Dijon mustard

Salt and pepper

Cook the macaroni in a large pot according the packet directions until al dente. Drain and return to the pot with the butter and mix through.

Add the remaining ingredients and mix together thoroughly. Season to taste.

Spoon two-third cup amounts of the mixture into the pie maker holes.

Close the lid and cook for 20 minutes until golden brown on top and cooked through.

MAKES 8 SMALL PIES

Spaghetti Muffins

230g spaghetti, broken into roughly 4cm lengths

2 tbsps butter

1 small onion, finely chopped

2 small cloves garlic, minced

¼ tsp cayenne pepper

1 cup (240ml) milk

1½ cups (185g) mixed grated cheese (such as mozzarella, Parmesan, tasty)

2 large eggs, lightly beaten

1 cup (165g) cooked broccoli, roughly chopped

1 cup (170g) cooked peas

Salt and pepper

Cook the spaghetti according to packet directions until al dente. Drain, toss with ½ tablespoon of the butter and set aside.

Heat the remaining butter in a large frying pan over medium heat. Fry the onion, garlic and cayenne for 5 minutes until softened. Remove from heat to a large mixing bowl.

Add the milk, cheese and egg to the onion and mix through. Add the broccoli, peas, spaghetti and mix together thoroughly. Season to taste.

Place two-third cup amounts of the mixture into the pie maker holes.

Close the lid and cook for 20 minutes until golden brown on top and cooked through.

MAKES 8 SMALL PIES

Hack it!

• *You can swap the broccoli and peas with equivalent amounts of capsicum, zucchini, tomato, corn or whatever's in the fridge. This is an ideal recipe for using up leftovers.*

Healthy Lentil Muffins

2 cups (300g) red lentil flour

2 tsps baking powder

¼ cup (30g) almond meal

½ cup (65g) pumpkin seeds

Pinch of salt

⅓ cup (80ml) butter, melted

3 medium eggs, lightly beaten

¼ cup (60ml) soy or almond milk

⅓ cup (40g) almonds, chopped, for topping

Mix together the dry ingredients in a large mixing bowl and make a well in the centre.

Beat together the butter, eggs, and milk.

Pour the wet ingredients into the well and mix until a thick batter forms.

Pour even amounts of the batter into each pie maker hole, filling each hole three-quarters full.

Sprinkle the chopped almonds over each muffin. Close the lid and cook for 12 minutes until golden brown on top or until a skewer inserted into the middle of one comes out clean.

MAKES 10

Broccoli Muffins

1 cup (125g) self-raising flour

1 cup (125g) wholemeal plain flour

2 tsps baking powder

2 cups (330g) small cooked broccoli florets

1 cup (250ml) milk

1 cup (125g) tasty cheese, grated

1½ tbsps fresh thyme leaves, chopped

1 large egg, lightly beaten

2 tbsps olive oil

Salt and pepper

Mix together the dry ingredients in a large mixing bowl and make a well in the centre.

In a separate bowl, combine the broccoli with the milk, cheese, thyme, egg, oil and a pinch each of salt and pepper.

Add the wet ingredients to the dry and mix until a thick batter forms.

Pour even amounts of the batter into each pie maker hole, filling each hole three-quarters full.

Close the lid and cook for 15 minutes until golden brown on top and cooked through.

MAKES 8

Leftovers Muffins

2 cups (330g) leftover cooked rice

250g leftover protein, such as chicken

⅔ cup (100g) leftover veggies such as spinach and carrot

1 cup (125g) mozzarella cheese, grated

¼ cup (10g) basil leaves, finely shredded

3 eggs, lightly beaten

Combine all the ingredients in a large mixing bowl. Stir well.

Spoon even amounts of the mixture into the holes of the pie maker.

Close the lid and cook for 10 minutes until golden brown on top.

MAKES 4-6

Quinoa and Cauliflower Muffins

1⅓ cups (250g) cooked quinoa

1 cup (165g) cauliflower, cooked and lightly mashed

1 small carrot, grated

½ cup (60g) tasty cheese, grated

1 tsp onion powder

1 tsp garlic powder

½ cup (20g) basil leaves, chopped

1 egg, beaten

Pinch of salt and pepper

5 cherry tomatoes, cut in half

Combine all the ingredients apart from the tomatoes in a large mixing bowl. Stir well.

Spoon even amounts of the mixture into the holes of the pie maker.

Press a cherry tomato half in the top of each muffin.

Close the lid and cook for 10 minutes until golden brown on top.

MAKES 10

Arancini

1 tbsp olive oil

1½ tsps chives, chopped

1 clove garlic, minced

1 cup (155g) Arborio rice

3 cups (800ml) chicken stock

½ cup (50g) Parmesan cheese, grated

1 egg, beaten

½ cup (125ml) buttermilk

1⅔ cups (205g) plain breadcrumbs

75g chicken-seasoned coating mix

200g mozzarella cheese, cut into small cubes

Heat the oil in a large pan over medium heat. Add the chives and garlic and fry for a minute until fragrant. Add the rice and stir a few times. Slowly begin adding the chicken stock, a good splash at a time, stirring until absorbed after each addition. Continue cooking like this for the next 20-25 minutes until stock has been used up and the rice still has a little bit of bite but is creamy. Top up with water if you run out of chicken stock.

Remove from the heat and stir in the Parmesan cheese. Set aside to cool slightly.

When cool, stir through the beaten egg.

Place the buttermilk in a shallow dish.

Place the breadcrumbs and chicken seasoning in a second shallow dish and mix together.

Take a small handful of risotto mixture, place an indent in it using your thumb and then press one or two pieces of mozzarella inside. Reform as a ball.

Dip the ball in the buttermilk, shaking off any excess. Then roll in the breadcrumb mix.

Brush the inside of the pie maker holes with oil. Place a ball in each hole. Close the lid and cook about 5-6 minutes, turning a few times during cooking to ensure an even browning.

MAKES 8-10

Zucchini Tarts

1½ sheets shortcrust pastry

2 zucchinis, sliced into matchsticks

½ tsp salt

1 tsp olive oil

1 cup (250ml) thickened cream

2 eggs, beaten

1 tbsp fresh parsley, chopped

2 tsps fresh chives, chopped

¼ tsp pepper

½ cup (60g) Cheddar, grated

Preheat oven to 190°C (375°F, Gas Mark 5) and line a baking tray with greaseproof paper.

Arrange zucchini on prepared tray in a single layer. Sprinkle with salt and drizzle with olive oil. Bake for 10 minutes, until softened and starting to brown.

Combine zucchini, cream, eggs, herbs and pepper in a medium bowl.

Cut six circles large enough for the base and sides of your pie holes, and place them into your pie maker. Pour mixture into pastry cases and sprinkle cheese on top.

Bake for 8 minutes, until filling is set and cheese is golden on top. Cool on a wire rack.

MAKES 6

Leek Tart

1 tbsp butter

4 leeks, chopped

1 tbsp dried dill (or use mixed herbs)

Pinch of salt

½ tsp salt

¾ cup (200ml) thickened cream

2 eggs, beaten

¼ tsp pepper

1 batch shortcrust pastry (see page 14)

½ cup (60g) Cheddar cheese, grated

Melt butter in a large saucepan over medium heat. Add leeks, dill and a pinch of salt. Cover and cook over medium-low heat for 5 minutes, until leeks have softened.

Combine cream, eggs, a third of the leeks and the pepper in a medium bowl.

Roll out the pastry to the desired thickness on a lightly floured workbench.

Using a sharp knife or the cutter provided, cut a large round from the pastry to fit the base and sides of your family pie maker. Press the pastry into the pie hole using fingers or a wooden spoon.

Pour mixture into the pastry base and place the Cheddar and remaining leeks on top.

Close the lid and cook for 8 minutes, until filling is set.

MAKES 1 FAMILY PIE

Vegetable Birds' Nests

2 carrots, peeled

1 onion, chopped

1 whole egg, plus 1 egg white, lightly beaten

2 tbsps Parmesan cheese, grated

2 tbsps plain flour

2 tbsps panko breadcrumbs

¼ tsp salt

Julienne the carrots using a sharp knife or a hand spiraliser if you have one. Place into a large mixing bowl with the onion. Add the eggs, cheese, flour, panko and salt. Gently toss the ingredients together.

Scoop spoonfuls of the mixture into the holes of the pie maker.

Close the lid and cook for 10 minutes until golden and the egg is set.

Rest for a minute and then remove with a heat-proof spatula.

MAKES 6-8

Baked Potato Pies

2 potatoes, for baking

1 tsp olive oil

¼ cup (25g) Parmesan cheese, finely grated

2 tbsps fresh dill, finely chopped (or 1 tbsp dried)

½ cup (125ml) cream

Preheat the oven to 190°C. Clean the potatoes and pat dry. Rub with a little olive oil and placed on a lined baking tray. Transfer to the oven to cook until just tender, approximately 45 minutes. Remove from the oven and set aside until cool enough to handle.

Meanwhile mix together the cheese (retaining a little for the tops), dill and cream in a small bowl.

Carefully remove the skin from the potatoes and discard it. Using a sharp knife slice the potato into thin pieces.

Place the potato slices into the holes of the pie maker, alternating each slice with a little of the cream mixture. Finish by sprinkling cheese on top of each pie.

Close the lid and cook for 8 minutes or until golden and cheese has melted.

MAKES 4 SMALL PIES

Tip:
• You can cook the jacket potatoes however you like. You might prefer to do them in the microwave or air fryer for speed.

Potato and Onion Pockets

2 small potatoes, diced

2 tbsps olive oil

3 spring onions, chopped

1 stalk celery, sliced

1 small zucchini, sliced

2 pita bread pockets

Boil the potatoes in a saucepan of lightly salted water until tender (or cook them in the microwave). Drain and set aside.

Meanwhile heat the oil in a large frying pan and cook the spring onion, celery and zucchini for 5 minutes or until softened, stirring occasionally. Mix together with the potatoes.

Spoon the potatoes and spring onion mixture into each pocket equally.

Place in a family pie maker, flattening slightly.

Cook for 10 minutes until golden.

MAKES 2 MEDIUM POCKETS

Tip:

• If you have time, these are great made with the two-ingredient dough on page 17.

Mushroom and Goat's Cheese Tart

Olive oil, for frying

200g mushrooms, chopped

Salt and pepper, to season

2 eggs, lightly beaten

225g goat's cheese

1 sheet shortcrust pastry

6 cherry tomatoes

Parsley leaves, to garnish

Heat oil in a frying pan over medium heat. Add the mushrooms and fry for 1 minute; season to taste.

In a mixing bowl combine eggs with goat's cheese. Fold in the mushrooms.

Using a sharp knife or the cutter provided, cut a large round from the pastry to fit the base and sides your family pie maker. Press in using fingers or a wooden spoon.

Fill the pastry with the mixture. Place the tomatoes on top.

Close the lid and cook for 7 minutes.

Let the tart rest for a minute and then remove with a plastic or wooden spatula and cool on a wire rack.

Garnish with parsley leaves to serve.

MAKES 1 FAMILY PIE

Cheesy Potato Scrolls

½ batch puff pastry (see recipe page 13) rolled out into two
24 x 24cm square sheets, 3mm thick

1½ tbsps olive oil

1 cup (150g) potato, grated, squeezed to remove excess liquid

1 cup (125g) tasty cheese, grated

½ tbsp garlic and herb seasoning (such as Masterfoods)

⅓ cup (15g) parsley, roughly chopped

Cut the pastry sheets into 3cm-thick strips. Lightly brush one side of each strip with oil.

Mix the potato, cheese, seasoning and parsley together in a mixing bowl until thoroughly combined.

Sprinkle the strips with the potato mixture. Carefully roll the strips up into loose spirals and tuck into the pie maker holes. (Transfer any uncooked scrolls to the refrigerator until ready to cook.)

Close the lid and cook for 30 minutes until cooked through and golden brown.

Remove the scrolls from the pie maker and sit on paper towels in a warm place until ready to eat.

MAKES 16

Easy Pizza Scrolls

250g pizza dough

½ cup (115g) pizza sauce

½ cup (130g) pesto

1 cup (120g) tasty cheese, grated

Roll out the dough and cut into two rectangular strips approximately 20cm long and 12cm wide.

Spread the strips with pizza sauce and then with pesto. Sprinkle with the cheese in equal amounts.

Starting at one short side, roll dough into a sausage shape. Slice each roll into four pieces. Place the slices, cut-side up, into pie maker holes.

Cook for 18-20 minutes, turning once or twice during cooking.

Let the scrolls rest for a minute and then remove with a plastic or wooden spatula and cool on a wire rack.

MAKES 8

Tip:
• *You can also make these with pastry and they are great for using up leftover strips.*

Hack it!
• *Try these scrolls with your favourite fillings such as ham and cheese, or cheese and Vegemite.*

Tomato Cheese Cups

½ tbsp olive oil

1 medium onion, finely chopped

4 Roma tomatoes, chopped

1 tsp ground oregano

½ tsp sugar

Salt and pepper

1 batch of shortcrust pastry (store-bought or see recipe page 14)

¾ cup (90g) tasty cheese, grated

¼ cup (30g) Parmesan cheese, grated

⅓ cup (15g) parsley, roughly chopped, to garnish

Heat the oil in a medium-sized frying pan over medium heat. Fry the onion for 5 minutes until softened. Add the tomatoes, oregano, sugar and a pinch each of salt and pepper. Fry for 15 minutes until thickened. Remove from heat and let cool for 20 minutes.

Roll out the pastry to the desired thickness on a lightly floured workbench. Using a sharp knife or the cutter provided, cut eight rounds from the pastry to fit the holes of your pie maker. Press the pastry into the pie holes using fingers or a wooden spoon. Heap with the tomato mixture.

Mix together the cheeses and sprinkle over the cups.

Close the lid and cook for 12 minutes until golden brown on top and the pastry is cooked. Serve garnished with parsley.

MAKES 8

Stuffed Rolls

4 small crusty bread rolls

1 tbsp oil

½ small onion, finely chopped

½ carrot, finely grated

1 small clove garlic, minced

200g pork mince

½ tsp cumin

1 tsp paprika

½ cup (60g) tasty cheese, grated

1 egg, beaten

1 tbsp milk

Cut down one side of each bread roll with a sharp knife. Gently prise the rolls open and remove some of the bread. Set aside the rolls and the bread filling.

Heat the oil in a large frying pan over medium heat and add the onion, carrot and garlic. Cook, stirring, for 3 minutes until soft. Add the mince and cook for a further 3-4 minutes until the meat is no longer pink. Add the cumin and paprika as well as about a tablespoon of the bread roll filling. Stir to combine and remove from the heat.

Scoop even amounts of the mixture into each hollowed out roll.

Squeeze the rolls into the pie maker. Mix the egg and milk together to make an egg wash. Using a pastry brush, apply the egg wash to the tops of the rolls.

Close the lid and cook for 5-7 minutes until golden.

MAKES 4

Tip:
• *Use shortcrust pastry, dough or pita pockets for this recipe if preferred.*

Keto Cheese Biscuits

3 tbsps coconut flour

2 tsps baking powder

½ tsp salt

¼ tsp xanthan gum

1 tsp agave syrup

2 medium eggs, lightly beaten

⅓ cup (80ml) milk

¾ cup (90g) mixed cheese, grated (such as mozzarella, Parmesan, tasty)

Salt and pepper

Mix together the dry ingredients and make a well in the centre.

Whisk together the syrup, eggs, milk, cheese and melted butter. Tip into the dry ingredients and mix thoroughly. Lightly season.

Place large dessertspoon amounts of mixture into the pie maker holes.

Close the lid and cook for 15 minutes until golden brown on top and cooked through.

MAKES 12

Keto Muffin Sandwiches

½ cup (110ml) coconut oil, melted

6 large eggs, lightly beaten

1¼ cups (125g) almond flour

¼ cup (25g) coconut flour

½ tsp salt

2 tsps baking powder

Mixed lettuce, to serve

4 slices cheese, to serve

200g shaved ham, to serve

Tomato sauce, to serve

Whisk together the coconut oil and eggs with the dry ingredients in a large bowl until completely mixed through and light and fluffy.

Drop ¼ cup amounts of mixture into the pie maker holes.

Close the lid and cook for 8 minutes until golden and cooked through.

Let cool for 5 minutes.

To make the sandwiches, place some lettuce on top of one muffin and layer with cheese, ham and sauce. Place another muffin on top and secure with a cocktail stick. Repeat with the remaining muffins and serve.

MAKES 8

Potato and Tuna Patties

1 cup (260g) mashed potato

⅓ cup (60g) peas, cooked

2 large eggs, lightly beaten

1 x 400g can tuna in spring water, drained and flaked

¼ cup (10g) parsley, chopped

1 tsp lemon juice

¼ tsp salt

¼ tsp pepper

1 cup (125g) breadcrumbs

Place the potato, peas, a third of the egg, tuna, parsley, lemon juice, salt and pepper in a large mixing bowl and stir to combine thoroughly.

Form into 10 patties. Place in the refrigerator for 30 minutes to firm.

Place the remaining egg in a shallow dish. Place the breadcrumbs in a separate shallow dish.

Dredge the patties in the egg and then coat in the breadcrumbs. Place the patties in the maker.

Close the lid, cook for 6 minutes. Flip the patties over with a silicon or wooden spatula and cook for another 6 minutes. Keep the cooked patties in a warm place while cooking the remaining patties.

MAKES 10

Chicken, Pea and Cheese Patties

300g chicken mince

1 cup (260g) mashed potato

⅔ cup (115g) peas, cooked

1 cup (125g) tasty cheese, grated

¼ cup (30g) breadcrumbs

1 medium egg, lightly beaten

1½ tsps chicken seasoning

1 tbsp mixed herbs

Place all the ingredients in a large bowl and mix together thoroughly.

Form into 12 small patties and place in the refrigerator to chill for 30 minutes.

Place the patties in the pie maker.

Close the lid and cook for 10 minutes, then flip the patties over with a silicon spatula and cook for another 10 minutes until cooked through.

Keep the cooked patties in a warm place on paper towels while cooking the remaining patties.

MAKES 12

Chicken Kiev

500g chicken mince

1 egg

1 tbsp + 1 cup (125g) panko breadcrumbs

90g butter

1 tbsp garlic, minced

30g parsley from a tube (such as Gourmet Garden Paste brand)

1 tbsp oil

Combine the chicken, egg and 1 tablespoon of panko in a large mixing bowl. Stir well.

Using clean hands, form into balls and set aside.

Mix the butter, garlic and parsley together and place in plastic wrap. Roll into a sausage shape and refrigerate for 1 hour or until firm. Then cut into slices.

Combine 1 cup panko with the oil in a shallow bowl.

Push a disc of butter mix into a chicken ball and reform the ball around it. Roll the ball in the panko mix. Repeat with all the balls.

Transfer the chicken balls into the pie holes, gently pressing them down. Close the lid.

Cook for 10 minutes, turning twice during cooking.

MAKES 6

Salmon Patties

1 x 425g tin salmon, drained and flaked

1 tsp dried mixed herbs

1 egg, lightly beaten

1 tsp Dijon mustard

1 tbsp capers, finely chopped

2 cups (520g) mashed potato

Pinch of salt and pepper

¾ cup (90g) breadcrumbs

Place all the ingredients apart from the breadcrumbs into a large mixing bowl and stir to combine, being careful not to break up the fish too much.

Form into 8 patties. Place in the refrigerator for 30 minutes to firm.

Place the breadcrumbs in a shallow bowl. Roll the patties in the breadcrumbs until well coated.

Place patties into pie maker holes. Cook for 10 minutes on both sides until golden brown.

MAKES 8

Mushroom Tofu Croquettes

2 large portobello mushrooms, chopped

2 eggs, beaten

1 cup (165g) cooked brown rice

½ cup (130g) silken tofu

1 tsp cumin

1 tbsp mixed dried herbs

½ cup (60g) almond flour

Salt and pepper

1 cup (125g) panko breadcrumbs

Put the chopped mushrooms into a bowl and add half the beaten egg. Add the rice, tofu, cumin, herbs and almond flour and combine well.

Using your hand, shape into patties.

Season the remaining egg with salt and pepper and then roll the patties in the egg mixture.

Place the panko in a shallow bowl. Roll the patties in the panko until well coated.

Place the patties in the holes of the pie maker and cook for 5 minutes each side until crisp and warmed through.

Let the croquettes rest for a minute and then remove with a plastic or wooden spatula and cool on a wire rack.

MAKES 4

Chicken Patties

500g chicken mince

¼ cup (40g) cornflour

1 egg white, lightly whisked

1 small onion, finely chopped

1 cup (125g) fresh white breadcrumbs

1 tbsp tomato sauce

1 tbsp barbecue sauce

2 tsps Worcestershire sauce

Salt and pepper

Place all of the ingredients into a large mixing bowl, or the bowl of a food processor, and stir (or process) until well combined.

With clean hands, roll mixture into small balls.

Press the patties into the holes of the pie maker and close the lid.

Cook for 8 minutes, turning halfway through cooking. Check after 6 minutes.

Let the patties rest for a minute and then remove with a plastic or wooden spatula.

MAKES 6

Mini Pizzas

250g two-ingredient dough (see page 17) or store-bought pizza dough ball

2 tbsps tomato paste (or ketchup)

4 cherry tomatoes, halved

8 mixed olives, sliced

¼ small zucchini, finely sliced

¼ cup (30g) mozzarella cheese, grated

Roll out the dough on a lightly floured surface and cut to fit your pie maker using a sharp knife or the cutter provided.

Spread each base with tomato paste (or ketchup) and place them into the pie maker.

Add the toppings, finishing with the grated cheese.

Close the lid and cook for 4 minutes until golden and cheese has melted.

MAKES 8

Tip:

• Make this kid-friendly by adding their favourite toppings, such as ham and pineapple or cheese and ham. And don't forget, these are lunchbox-friendly too.

Black Bean Papusa Pies

½ medium onion, minced

2 cloves garlic, minced

2 tbsps olive oil

1 x 400g can black beans, rinsed and drained

½ cup (125ml) vegetable stock (or use water)

½ tsp cumin

½ tsp smoked paprika

½ tsp mixed dried herbs

Pinch of salt and pepper

1 tsp lime juice

250g two-ingredient dough (see page 17) or store-bought pizza dough ball (or see tip below)

Fry the onion and garlic in olive oil in a large frying pan over medium heat for 3 minutes until softened. Add the black beans, stock, cumin, paprika, herbs and salt and pepper and cook for a further 5 minutes. Remove from the heat and use a potato masher to soften the beans into a paste. Return to the heat and simmer for around 5 minutes or until the liquid has evaporated. Stir in the lime juice and set aside to cool.

Taking around 3 tablespoons of dough, use your fingers to make a hole and work it until you form a little cup. Place 1 tablespoon of the bean mixture into the cup and close the top. Gently flatten between your hands. Keep going like this until you have used up all the dough and filling mixture.

Transfer the papusas with the seam-side down to the holes of the pie maker, gently pressing them in.

Cook for 10 minutes.

MAKES 6-8

Tip:

• For an authentic papusa dough combine 5 cups masa harina with 4 cups warm water.

Spinach and Ricotta Turnovers

1-2 sheets puff pastry

½ cup (125g) ricotta

½ cup (120g) feta, chopped or crumbled into small pieces

1 spring onion, finely sliced

½ cup (60g) tasty cheese, grated

150g frozen spinach, thawed

½ tsp salt

Pinch of pepper

¼ cup (35g) pine nuts (optional)

1 egg, beaten

1 tbsp milk

Sesame seeds, to garnish (optional)

Cut the pastry into four squares that are almost twice as big as the holes of your pie maker and set aside.

Combine the ricotta, feta, spring onion, tasty cheese, spinach, salt and pepper and pine nuts (if using) together in a mixing bowl.

Place the pastry squares into the pie maker holes with the edges hanging over. Spoon in the filling, then simply fold the corners of the pastry over the top to meet in the middle, almost covering the filling.

Mix the egg and milk to create an egg wash. Brush the pastry with the egg wash and sprinkle with sesame seeds if using.

Close the lid and cook for 8-10 minutes until golden.

MAKES 4

Pies and Fillings

Hearty BBQ Beef Pie

Oil, for frying

500g beef chuck steak, diced

200g brown mushrooms

1 onion, finely chopped

3 cloves garlic, crushed

1 tbsp plain flour

⅓ cup (80ml) barbecue sauce

1 tbsp Dijon mustard

1 cup (250ml) water

1 beef stock cube

Salt and pepper

6-7 sheets shortcrust pastry

1 egg, beaten

Heat a splash of oil in a large saucepan over a medium heat. Fry the beef for 3-5 minutes until browned, then set aside.

Add more oil in the same pan and cook the mushrooms for 2 minutes. Add the onion and garlic and cook, stirring until the onions have softened. Add the flour and cook, stirring for 1 minute.

Return the beef to the pan and add the barbecue sauce, mustard and water. Crumble in the stock cube and bring to the boil.

Reduce the heat and simmer, uncovered, for about 5 minutes or until sauce has thickened. Season and place in a bowl. Cool slightly, then pop in the fridge until cold.

Cut 24 circles from the shortcrust pastry sheets to fit your pie maker (note that the circles for the base and sides will need to be larger than those for the top).

Place the shortcrust pastry circles into the holes of the pie maker. Spoon the cooled filling into the holes.

Press the smaller circles on the top.

Brush with the lightly beaten egg.

Cook for 10 minutes or until the pastry is golden brown.

MAKES 12 SMALL PIES

Chilli Beef Pie Filling

Oil, for frying

500g beef mince

2 onions, finely chopped

1 capsicum, chopped

2 cloves garlic, minced

½ tsp ground cumin

1 tsp chilli powder

½ tsp smoked paprika

2 long green chillies, chopped

1 tsp tomato puree

½ cup (105ml) red wine

1 x 400g can diced tomatoes

½ cup (125ml) vegetable stock

½ cup (100g) corn kernels

1 x 400g kidney beans, drained

2 tbsps fresh oregano, chopped, or 2 tsps dried oregano

Salt and pepper

Heat a splash of oil in a large saucepan over a medium heat. Add the mince and fry, stirring, for 3-4 minutes until browned. Remove mince from the pan and set aside.

Heat the remaining oil in the same pan. Fry the onions for 3-4 minutes, stirring constantly. Add the capsicum and garlic and cook for 2 minutes. Return the meat to the pan.

Add the cumin, chilli, paprika and green chillies and fry for 1 minute until aromatic.

Add the tomato puree and fry for a further 1 minute.

Add the wine and turn up the heat for a minute to burn off the alcohol.

Add tomatoes, vegetable stock, corn, kidney beans and oregano. Add water, if needed. Season with salt and pepper and simmer on low to medium heat for 20 minutes.

MAKES 12 SMALL PIES

Easy Bolognaise Pie Filling

2 tbsps butter

1 onion, chopped

500g beef mince

1 carrot, finely chopped

2¼ cups (500g) tomato passata

Salt and pepper

Melt the butter in a frying pan and cook the onion, stirring, for 2 minutes. Add the mince and cook for a few minutes until browned.

Add remaining ingredients and bring to a boil. Reduce the heat and simmer for 20-30 minutes.

Add a little hot water or stock as needed to reach the desired consistency.

MAKES 8 SMALL PIES

Tip:

• *Replace the passata with a 420g can of tomato soup if you have it in the pantry.*

Savoury Mince Pie Filling

Oil, for frying

500g beef mince

1 onion, finely chopped

1 carrot, finely diced

1 stick celery, finely diced

2 cloves garlic, minced

1 tbsp dried oregano

2 tbsps tomato paste

½ cup (125ml) vegetable stock (or red wine)

1 x 400g can tomatoes

Heat a splash of oil in a large saucepan over a medium heat. Add the mince and fry, stirring, for 3-4 minutes until browned all over. Remove mince from the pan and set aside.

Heat a little more oil in the same pan. Add the onions and fry for 3 minutes, stirring constantly. Add carrot, celery and garlic and fry for a further 3 minutes. Return the meat to the pan. Add the oregano and fry for 1 minute until aromatic. Add the tomato paste and fry for a further 1 minute.

Add stock and tinned tomatoes. Season with salt and pepper, stir well and simmer for 20 minutes.

MAKES 12 SMALL PIES

Spicy Beef and Bean Pies

Oil, for frying

500g beef mince

2 onions, finely chopped

2 cloves garlic, minced

½ tsp ground cumin

2 tsps chilli flakes

1 tsp tomato puree

½ cup (105ml) red wine

1 x 400g can diced tomatoes

½ cup (125ml) vegetable stock

1 x 400g kidney beans, drained

2 tbsp fresh thyme leaves, or 2 tsps dried thyme

6-7 sheets shortcrust pastry

1 egg, beaten

Heat a splash of oil in a large saucepan over a medium heat. Add the mince and fry, stirring, for 3-4 minutes until browned all over. Remove from the pan and set aside.

Add more oil in the same pan. Fry the onions for 3-4 minutes, stirring constantly. Add the garlic and cook for 2 minutes. Return the meat to the pan. Add the cumin, chilli flakes and tomato puree and fry for a further 1 minute. Add the wine and turn up the heat for a minute to burn off the alcohol. Add tomatoes, vegetable stock, kidney beans and thyme. Simmer for 20 minutes. Set aside to cool.

Cut 24 circles from the shortcrust pastry sheets to fit your pie maker (note that the circles for the base and sides will need to be larger than those for the top).

Place the shortcrust pastry circles into the holes of the pie maker. Spoon the cooled filling into the holes.

Press the smaller circles on the top and brush with the lightly beaten egg.

Cook for 10 minutes or until the pastry is golden brown.

MAKES 12 SMALL PIES

Lebanese-Style Lamb Pie

⅓ cup (45g) pine nuts

Oil, for frying

250g lamb mince

1 small onion, minced

1 tomato, finely diced

1 tsp garlic

1 tsp sumac

½ tsp allspice (optional)

1 tsp salt, to taste

½ tsp freshly ground black pepper

½ lemon, juiced

3 sheets puff pastry

1 egg, beaten

1 tbsp milk

Place the pine nuts in a small frying pan over high heat and dry fry for 2-3 minutes, stirring constantly, until golden brown. Remove from the heat and set aside.

Heat a splash of oil in a large saucepan over a medium heat. Add the mince and fry, stirring, for 3-4 minutes until browned all over. Remove from the pan and set aside.

Place the onion, tomato, garlic, sumac, allspice, if using, salt and pepper and lemon juice in a large bowl and stir to combine. Add the mince and mix everything together well.

Place one sheet of pastry across the base and up the sides of a family pie maker. Spoon in half of the meat mixture and spread evenly across the pastry base. Layer on the next sheet of puff pastry and spoon over the remaining filling. Add the final piece of puff pastry. Close the pie by wrapping any overlapping pastry over the top and lightly pinch closed.

Mix the egg and milk to create an egg wash. Brush the pastry top with the egg wash, then close the lid of the pie maker and cook for 15 minutes until golden and meat is cooked through.

MAKES 1 FAMILY PIE

Steak and Vegetable Pie Filling

800g stewing beef, fat trimmed

2 tbsps olive oil

Salt and pepper

4 medium onions, peeled and quartered

3 cloves garlic, crushed

½ cup (125ml) red wine

2 tbsps tomato paste

1 tbsp fresh thyme, chopped

2 tbsps red wine vinegar

300g mushrooms, quartered

3 medium carrots, halved lengthways and sliced

500g white potatoes, cut into 3cm chunks

2 cups (500ml) beef stock

2 bay leaves

Preheat the oven to 170°C.

Toss the beef with half the oil and a good couple of grinds of salt and pepper.

Heat the rest of the oil in a large ovenproof casserole dish over medium heat. Fry the onion and garlic for 5 minutes. Add the beef and brown in batches, approximately 5 minutes for each batch. Remove each batch from the pan and set aside.

Pour the red wine into the pan and bring to a boil, stirring to remove any bits of meat from the bottom of the pan. Simmer for 2 minutes.

Add the tomato paste, thyme and vinegar and fry for a further 2 minutes.

Add the mushrooms, carrot and potato to the pot and cook for 5 minutes.

Return the beef to the pot and pour over the stock and add the bay leaves.

Bake in the oven for 2 hours until the beef is tender. Remove from oven and season to taste.

MAKES 2 FAMILY PIES

Steak and Cabbage Pie Filling

3 tbsps plain flour

Salt and pepper

500g round or gravy steak, cut into small chunks

2 tbsps olive oil

1 large onion, chopped

2 large cloves garlic, crushed

4 cups (400g) cabbage, chopped

1 tbsp dried mixed herbs

½ tsp chilli powder (optional)

1⅔ cups (400ml) vegetable stock

Season the flour and toss the beef in it to lightly coat.

Heat the oil in a large saucepan over medium heat. Fry the onion and garlic for 5 minutes until softened.

Add the beef and fry for 5 more minutes until the beef is browned.

Add the cabbage, herbs, chilli powder, if using, and stock and bring to a boil. Reduce to low and simmer, covered, for 2 hours until the beef is tender.

Season to taste and let cool before using as filling.

MAKES 12 SMALL PIES

Steak and Ale Pie Filling

¼ cup (30g) plain flour

Salt and pepper

700g chuck or gravy steak, cut into small chunks

2 tbsps olive oil

16 small pickling onions, peeled

3 large cloves garlic, crushed

1 medium potato, chopped

1⅔ cups (400ml) stout beer

¾ cup (200ml) beef stock

2 bay leaves

Salt and pepper

Season the flour and toss the beef in it to lightly coat.

Heat oil in a large deep-sided frying pan over medium heat. Fry the onions and garlic for 5 minutes until browned.

Add the beef and fry for 5 more minutes until the beef is browned.

Add the potato, beer, stock and bay leaves and bring to a boil. Reduce the heat to low and simmer, covered, for 2 hours until the beef is tender.

Season to taste and let cool before using as filling.

MAKES 12 SMALL PIES

Creamy Beef and Mushroom Pie Filling

300g round or gravy beef, cut into small chunks

6 tbsps plain flour

Salt and pepper

Olive oil, for frying

1 onion, finely chopped

455g mushrooms, sliced

3 cloves garlic, minced

1 tbsp fresh thyme leaves, chopped (or dried)

3 tbsps butter

1½ cups (375ml) beef (or vegetable) stock

1 tbsp lemon juice

½ cup (125ml) thickened cream

Preheat the oven to 160°C.

Season 3 tablespoons of the flour and toss the beef in it to lightly coat.

Heat a splash of oil in a large frying pan over medium heat. Add beef and fry for 3-4 minutes, stirring, until browned. Place in an ovenproof dish and set aside.

Heat more oil over a medium heat. Add onion and mushrooms and fry for 3-4 minutes until soft. Add garlic and thyme and fry for a further 1-2 minutes. Spoon the mixture over the beef.

In a medium saucepan over a high heat, melt the butter. Add the remaining 3 tablespoons of flour and cook, stirring constantly, until thick and lightly golden. Then add stock and lemon juice and whisk until smooth. Add cream and bring to a simmer.

Pour sauce over the beef and mushrooms. Cover with foil and place in the oven to bake for 45 minutes.

Season to taste and let cool before using as filling.

MAKES 1 FAMILY PIE

Steak and Mushroom Pie Filling

1 tbsp olive oil

1 large onion, chopped

3 tbsps plain flour

Salt and pepper

300g round or gravy beef, cut into small chunks

300g buttons mushrooms, quartered

2 small carrots, sliced

1 x 400g can diced tomatoes

¾ cup (200ml) tomato passata

1⅔ cups (400ml) beef stock

Heat the oil in a large saucepan over medium heat. Fry the onion for 5 minutes until softened.

Season the flour and toss the beef in it to lightly coat. Add the beef, mushrooms and carrots to the pan with the onion and fry for 5 minutes until the meat is browned.

Add the tomatoes, passata and stock and bring to a boil. Reduce heat to low and simmer, covered, for 2 hours until the beef is tender. Add more stock as needed.

Season to taste and let cool before using as filling.

MAKES 10 SMALL PIES

Slow-Cooked Lamb Taco Pie Filling

1kg boneless lamb shoulder

2 tsps lime zest

2 tbsps lime juice

2 tbsps brown sugar

1 tsp dried oregano

1 tsp cayenne pepper

1 tsp ground cinnamon

3 cloves garlic, crushed

2 tbsps olive oil

Preheat oven to 150°C. Place the lamb in a roasting dish.

In a medium bowl, mix together lime zest, 1 tablespoon lime juice, sugar, oregano, cayenne, cinnamon, garlic and olive oil. Rub the mixture over the lamb shoulder.

Place the lamb in the oven along with a small ovenproof bowl filled with 2cm water. Roast for 4 hours, ensuring that the small bowl always has a reserve of water. Remove the lamb from the oven and using two forks, shred the lamb.

MAKES 12 SMALL PIES

Tip:

• You can easily use this mixture to make pies. Pop a soft taco into the pie maker and spoon in the filling. Cook for 6-8 minutes.

Pulled Pork Pie Filling

2 tbsps olive oil

2 tbsps brown sugar

1 tsp ground cumin

1 tsp dried oregano

1 tsp ground coriander

1 tsp cayenne pepper

1 tsp salt

750g pork shoulder

1 onion, chopped

1 x 400g can diced tomatoes

Salt and pepper

Preheat oven to 150°C.

Mix half the oil with the sugar, cumin, oregano, coriander, cayenne and salt and use to coat the pork.

Roast the pork for 4 hours and keep an ovenproof bowl topped up with water in the oven the whole time.

Remove the pork from the oven, let cool for 20 minutes.

Use two forks to shred the pork. Reserve any liquid.

Heat the oil in a large frying pan over medium heat. Fry the onion for 10 minutes, then add the tomatoes and cook for 15 minutes. Add the pork and stir through.

Season to taste and let cool before using as filling.

MAKES 8 SMALL PIES

Tip:

• If you like you can cook the pork in the slow cooker for the 'set and forget' benefits. Place all the ingredients (plus 250ml chicken stock or water) in the slow cooker and cook on low for 6-8 hours until fork tender.

Pork and Mustard Pie Filling

Salt and pepper

⅓ cup (40g) plain flour

750g pork shoulder, trimmed and cut into 4cm strips

60g butter

1 small onion, finely chopped

3 large cloves garlic, crushed

¼ cup (60ml) dry white wine

2 cups (500ml) chicken stock

¾ cup (200ml) thickened cream

1 tbsp Dijon mustard

Season half the flour and toss the pork in it to coat.

Heat the butter in a large, deep-sided saucepan over medium heat. Fry the onion and garlic for 5 minutes until softened.

Add the pork and fry for 5 more minutes until browned. Add the wine and simmer until absorbed. Stir in the remaining flour for 1 minute. Add ¼ cup of the stock and stir through. Add the remaining stock and bring to a boil. Reduce heat to low and simmer, covered, for 1 hour.

Stir through the cream and mustard and bring to a simmer for 10 minutes, but do not let it boil.

Season to taste and let cool before using as filling.

MAKES 8 SMALL

Pork and Apple Pie

1 tbsp olive oil

1 small onion, finely chopped

400g pork mince

½ tbsp plain flour

2 medium apples, peeled and grated

2 tsps dried sage

¾ cup (180ml) chicken stock

Salt and pepper

1 batch shortcrust pastry (see recipe page 14)

Heat the oil in a medium-sized frying pan over medium heat. Fry the onion for 5 minutes until softened.

Add the pork and fry for 5 more minutes until browned. Stir through the flour for 1 minute, then add the apple and sage and stir through for 1 minute. Pour in the stock and bring to a boil. Reduce heat to low and simmer, covered, for 20 minutes.

Season to taste and let cool for 20 minutes.

Roll out the pastry to the desired thickness on a lightly floured workbench and use the pie cutter to cut out the pastry rounds.

Fit the larger round into the pie maker fill with the pork and apple filling. Place the top pastry round over the filling.

Close the lid and cook for 15 minutes until golden brown on top and cooked through.

MAKES 1 FAMILY PIE

Pork and Fennel Pie

1 tbsp oil

1 medium onion, finely chopped

2 cloves garlic, crushed

400g pork shoulder, trimmed and finely chopped

½ medium fennel bulb, chopped

1 tbsp fennel seeds

¼ cup (60ml) dry white wine

⅓ cup (80ml) chicken stock

1 batch shortcrust pastry (see recipe page 14)

Salt and pepper

Heat the oil in a medium-sized frying pan over medium heat. Fry the onion and garlic for 5 minutes until softened.

Add the pork, fennel and fennel seeds and fry for 5 more minutes until browned. Add the wine and simmer until absorbed. Add the stock and bring to a boil. Reduce heat to low and simmer, covered, for 20 minutes.

Season to taste and let cool for 20 minutes.

Roll out the pastry to the desired thickness on a lightly floured workbench and use the pie cutters to cut out the large and small pastry rounds.

Place the larger pastry rounds in the pie maker holes. Fill the pastry cases with filling level with the top of the pastry. Press the smaller rounds on top.

Close the lid and cook for 20 minutes until golden brown on top and cooked through.

MAKES 8 SMALL PIES

Pork, Sage and Onion Pie Filling

½ tbsp olive oil

2 medium onions, finely chopped

600g beef mince

200g pork mince

1 tsp dried sage

1½ tsps dried oregano

½ tsp ground mace

1 cup (240ml) vegetable stock

1½ cups (185g) breadcrumbs

Salt and pepper

Heat the oil in a large saucepan over medium heat. Fry the onion for 5 minutes until softened. Add the beef, pork, sage, oregano and mace and fry until the meat is browned. Drain any excess liquid.

Add the stock, then add the breadcrumbs, ½ cup at a time, until most of the stock is absorbed. Cook, covered, for 20 minutes. Season to taste and let cool before using as filling.

MAKES 10 SMALL PIES

Chicken and Tomato Pie Filling

1 tbsp olive oil

1 large onion, quartered and sliced

300g chicken breast, cut into bite-size chunks

300g chicken sausages, cut into 2cm pieces

1 x 400g can kidney beans, rinsed and drained

1 x 400g can diced tomatoes

¾ cup (200ml) tomato passata

1⅔ cups (400ml) chicken stock

1 tbsp cornflour

2 tbsps water

Salt and pepper

Heat the oil in a large saucepan over medium heat. Fry the onion for 5 minutes until softened.

Add the chicken and sausages to the pan with the onions and fry for 5 minutes until the meat is browned.

Add the beans, tomatoes, passata and stock and bring to a boil. Reduce heat to low and simmer for 20 minutes. Add more stock as needed.

Mix together the cornflour and water and stir into the stew for a few minutes until thickened.

Season to taste and let cool before using as filling.

MAKES 12 SMALL PIES

Tip:
• Make double the quantities so that you can enjoy a casserole one night and have filling for pies the next.

Creamy Chicken, Mushroom and Leek Pie Filling

2 tbsps olive oil

1 medium leek, thinly sliced

2 cloves garlic, crushed

400g chicken breast fillets, cut into chunks

200g button mushrooms, chopped

¼ cup (50ml) dry white wine

150ml chicken stock

25g butter

3 tsps dried marjoram

⅓ cup (100ml) thickened cream

½ batch of shortcrust pastry (see recipe page 14)

Salt and pepper

Heat the oil in a medium-sized frying pan over medium heat. Fry the leek and garlic for 5 minutes until softened. Add the chicken and fry for 6 minutes. Add the mushrooms and fry for a further 3 minutes. Turn the heat up to high and add the wine. Boil until evaporated, then reduce the heat to low and add stock and bring to a simmer. Cook for 20 minutes until all the liquid has evaporated. Stir through the cream and continue to heat through for a few minutes.

Season to taste, and let cool before using as filling.

MAKES 1 FAMILY PIE

Spicy Chicken Pie Filling

2 tbsps olive oil

1 small onion, finely chopped

2 cloves garlic, crushed

500g chicken thighs, cut into 1½ cm chunks

½ tbsp paprika

½ tbsp chilli flakes

1 x 400g can diced tomatoes

1 large red capsicum, chopped

1 tbsp flour

⅓ cup (100ml) chicken stock

¼ cup (10g) parsley, roughly chopped

Salt and pepper

Heat the oil in a large, deep-sided saucepan over medium heat. Fry the onion and garlic for 5 minutes until softened.

Add the chicken, paprika and chilli flakes and cook for 6 minutes. Add the tomatoes and capsicum and stir through for 2 minutes.

Mix together the flour and stock and drizzle into the pan, stirring continuously. Bring to a boil.

Reduce heat to a simmer and cook for 30 minutes. Stir through the parsley, season to taste and let cool before using for filling.

MAKES 8 SMALL PIES

Chicken, Mushroom and Bacon Pie Filling

2 tbsps olive oil

2-3 rashers thick-cut bacon

2 cloves garlic, crushed

400g chicken thigh fillets, cut into pieces

200g button mushrooms, chopped

¼ cup (50ml) dry white wine

150ml chicken stock

1 tbsp cornflour

2 tbsps water

25g butter

Salt and pepper

Heat the oil in a medium-sized frying pan over medium heat. Fry the bacon and garlic for 5 minutes until softened. Add the chicken and fry for 6 minutes. Add the mushrooms and fry for a further 3 minutes. Turn the heat up to high and add the wine. Boil until evaporated, then reduce the heat to low and add stock and bring to a simmer. Cook for 20 minutes until all the liquid has evaporated. Remove the mixture from the pan and set aside.

Mix together the cornflour and water and stir into the stew to thicken. Stir through the butter to finish.

Season to taste and allow to cool before using as filling.

MAKES 1 FAMILY PIE

Mexican Chicken and Sweetcorn Pie Filling

1 tbsp olive oil

1 large red onion, chopped

600g chicken breast, chopped

2 cups (350g) corn kernels

2 cups (400g) tomato, chopped

½ cup (125ml) chicken stock

2 tbsps fresh coriander, roughly chopped

½ tbsp ground oregano

2 tsps smoked paprika

1 tsp dried rosemary

¼ tsp cayenne pepper

Salt and pepper

Heat the oil in a large saucepan over medium heat. Fry the onion for 5 minutes until softened. Add the chicken and fry for a further 5 minutes. Stir through the remaining ingredients and bring to a boil.

Reduce heat to a simmer and cook for 30 minutes.

Season to taste and let cool before using as filling.

MAKES 8 SMALL PIES

Country Chicken Pie Filling

2 tbsps butter

1 small onion, finely chopped

600g chicken breast, chopped

1 small carrot, finely chopped

1 cup (170g) peas, fresh or frozen

1 tbsp cornflour

⅔ cup (150ml) chicken stock

1 tsp Dijon mustard

½ tbsp ground oregano

⅓ cup (100ml) cream

Salt and pepper

Heat the butter in a large frying pan over medium heat. Fry the onion for 5 minutes until softened. Add the chicken and fry for 8 minutes.

Stir in the carrot and peas for 2 minutes.

Mix together the cornflour and 2 tablespoons stock and drizzle into the pan, stirring continuously. Stir through the mustard and oregano.

Pour in the remaining stock and bring to a boil, stirring for 15 minutes until thickened.

Reduce the heat to low and stir through the cream.

Season to taste and let cool before using as filling.

MAKES 1 FAMILY PIE

White Fish and Dill Pie Filling

2 medium potatoes, peeled and cut into 1cm cubes

2 tbsps butter

2 medium spring onions, chopped

500g white fish fillets (such as snapper, tilapia or flat head), cut into small chunks

200g creme fraiche (or sour cream)

2 tbsps cornflour

¾ cup (200ml) milk

2 tbsps fresh dill, chopped

1 tsp lemon zest

Salt and pepper

Boil the potato for 12 minutes until just tender. Drain and set aside.

Heat the butter in a large frying pan over medium heat. Fry the spring onion for 3 minutes until softened. Add the fish and fry for 2 minutes until just cooked through.

Stir in the creme fraiche and potatoes and cook for 2 minutes.

Mix the cornflour with 2 tablespoons of the milk and drizzle over the mixture, stirring gently. Pour in the rest of the milk with the dill and zest and stir until thickened.

Season to taste and let cool before using as filling.

MAKES 1 FAMILY PIE

Spicy Prawn Curry Pie Filling

1½ cups (375ml) boiling water

2 chicken stock cubes

60g butter (or ghee)

1 onion, chopped

1½ tbsps curry powder

4 tbsps flour

1 cup (250ml) coconut cream

1 tbsp lemon juice

1 tsp brown sugar

500g raw prawns (fresh or frozen)

Combine the boiling water and stock cubes in a jug and stir. Set aside until dissolved.

Melt the butter or ghee in a frying pan over medium heat. Add the onion and curry powder and fry, stirring, for 3 minutes or until softened. Add the flour and stir until it is mixed through.

Empty the coconut cream into the jug with the stock and begin to gradually add it to the curry, stirring as you do so. Bring to the boil, stirring, until thickened.

Reduce the heat and stir through the lemon juice and sugar. Cook on a low heat for 20 minutes.

Add prawns and cook for further 2 minutes.

MAKES 1 FAMILY PIE

Tip:

• *You can substitute regular cream or milk for the coconut cream if that's what you have on hand.*

Salmon and Chive Pies

30g butter

½ cup (60g) plain flour

2 cups (500ml) milk

1 cup (125g) tasty cheese, grated

1 small smoked salmon fillet (or use a can of smoked salmon slices), cut into bite-sized pieces

1 hard-boiled egg, peeled and chopped

1 tbsp fresh chives, chopped

1 sheet puff pastry, cut into quarters

To make the cheese sauce first melt the butter in a small saucepan over medium heat. Add the flour and stir well. Slowly and gradually add the milk, stirring constantly to avoid lumps. Add half of the cheese and stir until just melted. Remove from the heat and set aside.

Mix together the fish, egg and chives in a medium-sized bowl. Add the cheese sauce and stir to combine everything. Allow to cool slightly.

Take a puff pastry square and place it in the palm of your hand. Place 2 tablespoons of the fish mixture into it and close the pastry around it. Flatten slightly by gently squeezing it between your hands.

Transfer the pies with the seam-side down to the holes of the pie maker, gently pressing them in.

Cook for 10 minutes.

MAKES 4 SMALL PIES

Tip:

• *Instead of making the cheese sauce from scratch, you could buy a store-bought sauce such as the Gravox cheese finishing sauce.*

Potato Top Pie

3 potatoes, peeled and cut into chunks

¼ cup (60ml) milk

30g butter

½ cup (60g) plain flour

2 cups (500ml) milk

1 cup (125g) tasty cheese, grated

1 kg thawed marinara mix (or use frozen seafood salad)

¼ cup (10g) fresh parsley, chopped

½ cup (50g) Parmesan cheese, finely grated

Bring potatoes to the boil in a pan of salted water. Cook until tender, about 15 minutes. Drain and return to the pan. Add the ¼ cup milk and mash until soft and creamy.

To make the cheese sauce first melt the butter in a small saucepan over medium heat. Add the flour and stir well. Slowly and gradually add the 2 cups milk, stirring constantly to avoid lumps. Add half of the tasty cheese and stir until just melted. Remove from the heat and set aside.

Add the marinara mix and the chopped parsley to the cheese sauce and stir to combine.

Scrape the seafood mixture into the pie maker. Spoon on the potato and sprinkle with the Parmesan cheese.

Close the lid and cook for 10 minutes until golden.

MAKES 2 FAMILY PIES

Salmon Pie

3 large potatoes, peeled and thinly sliced

200g creme fraiche (or sour cream)

½ cup (60g) tasty cheese, grated

2 tbsps olive oil

1 large onion, chopped

1 tsp fennel seeds

600g salmon fillet, roughly chopped

2 tsps Dijon mustard

1 tsp lemon zest

1 tbsp cornflour

1¼ cups (300ml) milk

300g baby spinach, roughly chopped

1 sheet puff pastry

Salt and pepper

Steam the potatoes for 10 minutes until nearly tender. Mix them with half the creme fraiche and the cheese. Set aside.

Heat the oil in a large saucepan over medium heat. Fry the onion for 5 minutes until softened. Add the fennel seeds and salmon and fry for 4 minutes until the salmon is just cooked.

Stir through the mustard and zest for 1 minute.

Mix the cornflour with 2 tablespoons of the milk and drizzle over the mixture, stirring gently. Pour in the rest of the milk and bring to a simmer. Reduce heat to low until the mixture thickens. Stir in the spinach and the rest of the creme fraiche. Reheat to a simmer, season to taste and let cool.

Using a sharp knife or the cutter provided, cut a cirlce from the pastry to fit a family pie maker. Press the puff pastry into the base of the pie maker and fill with the salmon filling. Spread the potato mixture over the top of the filling.

Close the lid and cook for 25 minutes until golden brown on top and cooked through.

MAKES 1 FAMILY PIE

Spicy Tomato and Chickpea Pie Filling

1 tbsp olive oil

1 onion, chopped

3 cloves garlic, minced

Medium piece of ginger, finely chopped

1 red capsicum, diced

2 tsps garam masala

1 tsp cumin

1 tsp hot chilli powder

¼ tsp cayenne pepper

1 x 400g can chickpeas, drained and rinsed

2 x 400g cans chopped tomatoes

Heat olive oil in a large saucepan over medium-high heat. Add the onion and fry for 5 minutes, until soft. Add the garlic and ginger and cook for a couple of minutes more, stirring frequently.

Add the capsicum and cook for 3-5 minutes until it starts to soften.

Add the garam masala, cumin, hot chilli powder and cayenne pepper, and stir to coat with the spices. Cook for 1-2 minutes until spices are aromatic.

Add the chickpeas and stir well so they are covered in oil and spice. Add the tomatoes and stir, then reduce heat to medium-low and allow to simmer gently for 20 minutes.

Season to taste and let cool before using as filling.

MAKES 1 FAMILY PIE

Vegetarian Potato Pie

2 medium potatoes, peeled and cut into 1cm cubes

1 tbsp olive oil

1 small onion, finely chopped

3 large cloves garlic, crushed

8 large eggs, lightly beaten

1 small bunch asparagus, cut into 3cm lengths

¾ cup (185ml) milk

1½ cups (185g) cheese, grated

⅓ cup (15g) parsley, roughly chopped

¼ tsp nutmeg

¼ tsp cayenne pepper

1 batch shortcrust pastry (see recipe page 14)

Salt and pepper

Steam the potatoes for 10 minutes until nearly tender. Set aside.

Heat oil in a large deep-sided frying pan over medium heat. Fry the onions and garlic for 5 minutes until browned. Remove to a large mixing bowl. Add the potatoes to the bowl when cooled slightly.

Add the remaining ingredients except the pastry to the mixing bowl with a pinch each of salt and pepper and mix thoroughly.

Roll out the pastry to the desired thickness on a lightly floured workbench. Cut out pie bases with the larger cutter.

Fill the cases with filling to two-thirds full. Fold the edges of the cases over onto the filling.

Close the lid and cook for 20 minutes until golden brown on top and cooked through.

Serve hot or cold.

MAKES 1 FAMILY PIE

Mushroom and Potato Pie Filling

2 small potatoes, peeled and chopped

Olive oil, for frying

½ onion, finely chopped

300g mushrooms, sliced

1 clove garlic, minced

3 tbsps butter

3 tbsps plain flour

1 cup (250ml) chicken (or vegetable) stock

1 tbsp lemon juice

¼ cup (60ml) thickened cream

Boil the potatoes in salted water until just cooked. Drain and set aside.

Heat oil in a medium saucepan over a medium heat. Add onion and mushrooms and cook for 3-4 minutes until soft. Add garlic and cook for a further 1-2 minutes. Set aside.

In the same saucepan, melt the butter. Add the flour and cook, stirring constantly, until thick and lightly golden. Then add stock and lemon juice and whisk until smooth. Add cream and bring to a simmer. Add the mushrooms and potatoes to the sauce and stir to combine.

Remove from the heat and allow to cool before using as filling.

MAKES 6 SMALL PIES

No-Meat Pie Filling

400g textured vegetable protein (TVP)

2 cups (500ml) boiling water

2 'beef style' vegan stock cubes (such as Massel)

½ cup (15g) vegan gravy granules (such as Goldenfry Smooth and Rich beef)

1 cup (250ml) hot water

1 tbsp olive oil

1 onion, diced

1 tbsp dried mixed herbs

400g tin chopped tomatoes

2 tbsps tomato paste

Place the TVP in a large bowl. Cover with the boiling water and set aside to soak.

Place the stock cubes and gravy granules in a jug and add the hot water. Set aside to dissolve.

Heat the olive oil in a large frying pan. Add the onion and herbs and fry for 3 minutes until softened. Add the chopped tomatoes and tomato paste and stir through.

Add the TVP and stock to the pan. Stir well and cook for 10 minutes, stirring frequently. Add a little more water if needed to achieve the desired consistency.

Remove from the heat and allow to cool before using as filling.

MAKES 1 FAMILY PIE

Tip:

• *TVP, Massel Beef Style stock cubes and Goldenfry gravy granules are available at most major supermarkets.*

Eggplant and Apple Pie Filling

Olive oil, for frying and drizzling

1 tsp fennel seeds

1 tsp cumin seeds

1 large eggplant, cut into small cubes

1 large Honey Crisp or Golden Delicious apple, unpeeled, cored, cut into 6

1 tsp salt

1 tbsp coriander, chopped

½ tsp ground cumin

1 carrot, finely diced

1 onion, chopped into quarters

1 stalk celery, finely diced

225g mushrooms, chopped

1 tbsp parsley, chopped

½ cup (115ml) water

Preheat the oven to 200°C.

Heat some oil in a frying pan over a high heat. Toss in the fennel seeds and whole cumin seeds. Fry them, stirring, for about 15 seconds.

Add the eggplant and apple. Sprinkle in the salt, coriander and ground cumin. Cook for 3-5 minutes, stirring often to incorporate the seasoning.

Transfer the contents to an ovenproof pan and add the carrot, onion, celery and mushrooms.

Liberally drizzle with olive oil and place in the oven for 20 minutes, tossing half way.

Season with more salt to taste and garnish with parsley.

Remove from the heat and allow to cool before using as filling.

MAKES 1 FAMILY PIE

Spicy Bean Pie Filling

2 tbsps olive oil

1 small onion, chopped

1 clove garlic, minced

1 x 400g can cannellini beans, drained

1 x 400g can chopped tomatoes

½ tsp smoked paprika

1 tsp ground cumin

1 tsp hot chilli powder

¼ tsp cayenne pepper

1 tbsp lemon juice

½ cup (125ml) vegetable stock

Salt and pepper

In a frying pan heat the olive oil over medium-high heat.

Add the onion and garlic and cook for 5 minutes, stirring frequently until the onion is softened.

Add the beans, tomatoes, spices, lemon juice and stock, as well as a couple of good grinds of salt and pepper, and stir through.

Bring to the boil, then reduce heat and simmer, covered, for 20 minutes, stirring occasionally.

Season to taste and let cool before using as filling.

MAKES 6 SMALL PIES

Tomato and Tofu Pie Filling

1 tbsp olive oil

1 small onion, chopped

2 small cloves garlic, minced

2 tsps ground cumin

600g tofu, cut into 1cm cubes

1 medium yellow capsicum, chopped

1 small zucchini, chopped

1 x 400g can crushed tomatoes

⅓ cup (15g) parsley, roughly chopped

½ cup (120ml) vegetable stock

Salt and pepper

Heat oil in a large deep-sided frying pan over medium heat. Fry the onion, garlic and cumin for 5 minutes until browned. Add the tofu, capsicum and zucchini and fry for another 5 minutes.

Add the tomatoes, parsley and stock and a pinch each of salt and pepper and bring to a boil. Reduce heat to a simmer and cook for 15 minutes until most of the liquid is absorbed.

Season to taste and let cool before using as filling.

MAKES 8 SMALL PIES

Spiced Eggplant, Lentil and Spinach Pie Filling

½ cup (90g) yellow lentils

2 cups (500ml) water

2 tbsps butter

1 small onion, finely chopped

2 large cloves garlic, crushed

2 tsps fresh ginger, finely grated

2 tbsps garam masala

1 small chilli, seeded and finely chopped

250g eggplant, finely chopped

300g baby spinach, roughly chopped

1 cup (200g) tomatoes, chopped

⅓ cup (15g) coriander, roughly chopped

⅔ cup (150ml) vegetable stock

Salt and pepper

Rinse the lentils and remove any grit or lentils that float.

Place the lentils in a pot with the water. Bring to a boil, then reduce the heat to low and simmer for 30 minutes. Drain and rinse the lentils and set aside.

Heat the butter in a large frying pan over medium heat. Fry the onion and garlic for 5 minutes until softened. Add the ginger, garam masala and chillies and fry for 1 minute.

Stir through the lentils and remaining ingredients and bring to a boil. Reduce heat to a simmer and cook, covered, for 15 minutes until most of the liquid has been absorbed.

Season to taste and let cool before using as filling.

MAKES 8 SMALL PIES

Curried Lentil Pie Filling

1 tbsp vegetable oil

2 tsps black mustard seeds

1 medium onion, finely diced

2-3 cloves garlic

2½ tsps ground cumin

1 tsp garam masala

2-3 bay leaves

1 tbsp tomato paste

5 cups (1.25L) vegetable stock

1½ cups (275g) yellow lentils, rinsed

2 tbsps ginger, grated

2 tsps turmeric

½ lemon, juiced

Heat the oil in a small saucepan on a medium-high heat. Add the mustard seeds. When they start to pop, add the onion and garlic and cook until just brown. Add the cumin, garam masala, bay leaves and tomato paste. Cook for another 2-3 minutes and set aside.

Place the vegetable stock in a large saucepan. Add the lentils, ginger and turmeric. Boil for 20 minutes until just tender. Place a stick blender in the pan and whizz for 5-10 seconds to create an uneven consistency, or remove 1 cup of the lentils from the pan and puree before returning to the pan. The mix should have a good texture with some full lentils and some thick sauce.

Add the spiced onion mixture to the pot of lentils. Cook over a low heat for another 15-20 minutes.

Finally add the lemon juice and stir thoroughly.

MAKES 1 FAMILY PIE

Sweets and Treats

Custard Buns

1 batch 2-ingredient dough (sweetened), see page 17

100g instant vanilla pudding mix (such as Aeroplane)

1¼ cups (300ml) thickened cream

⅔ cup (150ml) milk

Desiccated coconut, to serve

Combine the pudding mix, cream and milk using an electric mixer and chill for 1 hour.

Using a sharp knife or the cutter provided, cut six rounds from the dough to fit the holes of the pie maker. Press the dough into the pie holes using fingers or a wooden spoon.

Spoon in generous quantities of custard mix.

Close the pie maker lid and cook for 5 minutes, until the pastry begins to golden.

Dust with coconut and serve.

MAKES 6

Anzac Biscuits

2 cups (180g) rolled oats

¼ cup (20g) desiccated coconut

½ cup (80g) brown sugar

¾ cup (90g) plain flour

125g butter

1 tbsp golden syrup

1 tsp bicarbonate of soda

2 tbsps boiling water

Place the oats, coconut, sugar and flour in a mixing bowl and stir to combine.

Melt the butter in a small saucepan over medium heat (or use the microwave).

Combine the golden syrup, bicarb and boiling water in a second mixing bowl. When the mixture is frothing add the melted butter and quickly stir.

Pour the wet mixture into the dry ingredients and stir well to thoroughly combine.

Drop the biscuit mix in spoonfuls into the pie maker holes and lightly press down to flatten.

Cook for 7 minutes, checking after 5 minutes.

Let the biscuits rest for a minute and then remove with a plastic or wooden spatula. Place on a wire rack to cool.

MAKES 18

Gluten-Free Raspberry Friand

4 egg whites

⅔ cup (100g) icing sugar + extra for dusting

1 cup (125g) almond meal

⅓ cup (50g) gluten-free flour

1 tsp lemon juice

80g butter, melted

¾ cup (100g) raspberries

Whisk the egg whites until they become a white and frothy.

Combine the sugar, almond meal, flour and lemon juice in a mixing bowl.

Fold the eggs and butter mixture into the dry ingredients.

Gently incorporate the raspberries.

Spoon the batter into the pie holes.

Close the pie maker lid and cook for 8 minutes.

Dust with icing sugar to serve.

MAKES 4

Easy Cinnamon Scrolls

1 cup (250ml) Greek yoghurt

2 cups (250g) self-raising flour

100g soft butter

½ cup (110g) sugar

4 tsps cinnamon

⅓ cup (50g) raisins or sultanas (optional)

Make the dough by combining the flour and yoghurt.

Flour a work surface and knead the dough for 5 minutes.

Roll the dough into a large, 1cm-thick rectangle.

Spread the butter over the dough.

Sprinkle the sugar, cinnamon and sultanas or raisins, if using, evenly over the dough.

Roll the dough up into a scroll.

Cut the dough into 5cm sections.

Place the dough sections standing up in the pie maker holes.

Close the pie maker lid and cook for 8 minutes.

MAKES 4

Plum Pies

700g jar or can of whole plums in juice

1 tsp sugar

2 tbsps cornflour

1 sheet shortcrust pastry

Cut four plums into eighths.

Pour the plum juice and sugar into a small saucepan set over medium heat and bring to the boil. Add the cornflour and continue to cook for 2-3 minutes, stirring continuously, until thickened. Set aside to cool slightly.

Using a sharp knife or the cutter provided, create circles from the sheet of shortcrust pastry to fit the holes of pie maker.

Press the pastry into the pie holes using fingers or a wooden spoon.

Pour the plum syrup over each pastry base in equal measure and then top each with eight plum segments.

Push the corners of the pastry case over to slightly cover the filling.

Cook for 5 minutes until pastry begins to brown.

Let the pies rest for a minute and then remove with a plastic or wooden spatula.

MAKES 4

Plum Puffs

700g jar or can of whole plums in juice

1 tsp sugar

2 tbsps cornflour

1 sheet puff pastry

Icing sugar, to serve

Cut four plums in half and set aside.

Pour the juice and sugar into a small saucepan set over medium heat and bring to the boil. Add the cornflour and continue to cook for 2-3 minutes, stirring continuously, until thickened. Set aside to cool slightly.

Using a sharp knife or the cutter provided, create circles from the sheet of puff pastry to fit the holes of pie maker.

Press the pastry into the pie holes using fingers or a wooden spoon.

Cook for 4 minutes until puffed and lightly golden.

Let the pastry puffs rest for a minute and then remove with a plastic or wooden spatula.

Pour the plum syrup over each pastry puff in equal measure and then top with two plum halves.

Dust with icing sugar to serve.

MAKES 4

Tip:

• You will not need to use all the plums in the jar, but you will need to use all of the juice. Store the remaining plums in a container in the fridge for future use.

Festive Mince Pies

200g mixed fruit, roughly chopped

2 tbsps golden syrup

½ tsp cinnamon

½ tsp ground ginger

¼ tsp nutmeg

½ tsp allspice

1 small orange, zested

¼ cup (60ml) brandy

1 sheet shortcrust pastry

2 tsps icing sugar, to serve

Combine the mixed fruit, syrup, spices, orange zest and brandy in a bowl and place in the fridge to soak overnight.

Using a sharp knife or the cutter provided, create circles from the sheet of shortcrust pastry to fit the holes of the pie maker.

Re-roll the excess pastry and cut out small stars using a cookie cutter.

Press the pastry circles into the pie holes using fingers or a wooden spoon.

Fill the cases with the fruit mixture.

Place the pastry stars on top and close the pie maker lid.

Cook for 7 minutes.

Once cool, dust with icing sugar and serve.

MAKES 4 SMALL PIES

Apple and Raspberry Pies

600g apples, cooked

2½ cups (300g) raspberries

¼ cup (55g) sugar

2 sheets shortcrust pastry

1 tbsp cinnamon sugar

Place the apples, raspberries and sugar in a blender and gently blend until you have a chunky mixture.

Using a sharp knife or the cutter provided, create eight circles from the sheets of shortcrust pastry to fit the holes of pie maker (note that the circles for the bases will need to be slightly larger than those for the tops).

Press the pastry into the pie holes using fingers or a wooden spoon.

Spoon 2-3 teaspoons of apple and raspberry mixture into each case.

Place a pastry lid on each of the pies and sprinkle with cinnamon sugar.

Close the pie maker lid and cook for 5 minutes until golden brown.

MAKES 4 SMALL PIES

Chocolate Tarts

¾ cup (200ml) thickened cream

200g plain chocolate, broken into chunks

50g butter, softened

2½ tbsps sugar

1 sheet shortcrust pastry

1 tsp sea salt flakes

Heat the cream in a pan until it begins to simmer.

Place the chocolate and butter into a heatproof bowl.

Pour the hot cream and sugar over the chocolate and butter.

Stir the mixture until ingredients have fully melted.

Using a sharp knife or the cutter provided, create circles from the sheet of shortcrust pastry to fit the holes of the pie maker.

Press the pastry circles into the pie holes using fingers or a wooden spoon.

Fill the case with the chocolate ganache mixture.

Cook for 6 minutes.

Remove from the pie maker and sprinkle with sea salt.

Place the pies in the refrigerator for 2-3 hours to set.

MAKES 4 SMALL PIES

Hack it!

• If you don't fancy making a chocolate ganache, then go the even easier option. Place the contents of a tin of condensed milk, a packet of chocolate chips and 50g of butter in a bowl. Microwave for 1 minute. Stir well. Use this sauce to fill the pastry cases.

Chocolate Brownies

¾ cup (125g) dark chocolate chips

125g unsalted butter, chopped

1¼ cups (250g) sugar

1 cup (130g) plain flour

⅓ cup (40g) cocoa powder

1 tsp vanilla

2 eggs, lightly whisked

4 squares dark chocolate

Put the chocolate chips and butter in a pan and gently melt over low heat until glossy, then let cool slightly.

Combine the sugar, flour, cocoa and vanilla in a bowl.

Whisk the eggs into the cooled chocolate mixture.

Add the wet ingredients to the bowl of dry ingredients and mix.

Pour the brownie mix into the pie holes and then press a square of dark chocolate into the top of each brownie.

Cook for 7-8 minutes.

Once cooled, remove from the pie maker.

MAKES 4

Hack it!

• *Try making these with a chocolate brownie packet mix. Place in the pie maker and insert your favourite chocolate (mini Flake or mini Mars, for example) in the middle before cooking.*

Snow Cakes

300g cake mix

½ cup (125ml) lemonade

¾ cup (200ml) double cream, whipped

2 tsps icing sugar, to serve

Carefully combine the cake mix and the lemonade.

Pour half the batter into the pie holes.

Close the lid and cook for 4 minutes.

Once cool, remove the cakes from the pie maker and set aside.

Pour the remaining batter into the pie holes, close the lid and cook for 4 minutes.

Once cool, remove these cakes from the pie maker.

Generously spread the base of the cakes with cream and sandwich together.

To serve, dust with icing sugar.

MAKES 4

Chocolate Whoopie Pies

50g butter, softened

½ cup (100g) sugar

½ tsp vanilla

1 small egg, beaten

¾ cup (100g) plain flour

½ cup (50g) cocoa powder

½ tsp bicarbonate of soda

⅓ cup (100ml) buttermilk

¾ cup (200ml) double cream, whipped

Chocolate flavoured topping, to decorate

2 tsps icing sugar, to serve

Mix together the butter, sugar, vanilla and egg.

Gradually add the flour, cocoa powder, bicarb and buttermilk.

Pour half the batter into the pie holes.

Close the lid and cook for 4 minutes.

Once cool, remove the cakes from the pie maker and set aside.

Pour the remaining batter into the pie holes, close the lid and cook for 4 minutes.

Once cool, remove these cakes from the pie maker.

Generously spread the base of the cakes with cream and sandwich together.

To serve, decorate with chocolate topping and dust with icing sugar.

MAKES 4

Cottage Cheese Pancakes

¼ cup (55g) cottage cheese

1 egg, beaten

½ tsp baking powder

¼ cup (20g) oats

1 tsp sugar + extra, to serve

In a food processor, blend together the cottage cheese, egg, baking powder, oats and sugar.

Scrape the batter into the pie holes.

Close and cook for 6 minutes, flipping halfway through cooking.

Once cool, remove from the pie maker and set aside.

To serve, sprinkle with a little sugar.

MAKES 4

Jam Doughnuts

½ cup (60g) self-raising flour

¼ cup (55g) sugar

30g butter, melted

⅓ cup (80ml) milk

1 egg, beaten

½ tsp vanilla

½ cup (160g) raspberry jam

2 tsps icing sugar, to serve

Combine the flour and sugar in a large bowl.

In another bowl, whisk the butter, milk, egg and vanilla.

Slowly incorporate the wet ingredients into the dry, mixing thoroughly.

Place 2-3 tablespoons of mixture into the pie holes.

Drop a heaped teaspoon of jam into the centre of the batter.

Cover the jam with another spoon of the batter.

Close the lid and cook for 7 minutes.

Once cool, remove the doughnuts from the pie maker and dust with icing sugar.

MAKES 4

Vanilla Cheesecakes with Fruit

80g digestive biscuits, crushed

40g butter, melted

1 tbsp cornflour

3 tbsps sugar

250g cream cheese

1 egg

2 tbsps thickened cream

½ tsp vanilla

¼ tsp lemon zest

20 glace cherries

4 blackberries

Combine the digestive crumbs and butter in a mixing bowl until crumbs are well coated with the butter.

In a separate bowl, mix together the cornflour, sugar and cream cheese. Gradually add the egg, cream, vanilla and lemon zest, whisking the whole time.

Press 3-4 teaspoons of the biscuit crumb mixture into each hole to adequately cover the base.

Place 2-3 tablespoons of cheesecake mix on top of each biscuit base.

Close the pie maker lid and bake for 10 minutes.

Once cool and removed from the pie maker garnish with the cherries and blackberries.

MAKES 4

Lemon Curd Tarts

¾ cup (185ml) lemon juice

¼ cup (25g) lemon zest

½ cup (110g) sugar

3 eggs

6 tbsps unsalted butter

1 sheet shortcrust pastry

Place the juice, zest, sugar, eggs and butter in a pan and cook over a low heat for 10 minutes, or until thick.

Using a sharp knife or the cutter provided, create circles from the sheet of shortcrust pastry to fit the holes of the pie maker.

Press the pastry into the pie holes using fingers or a wooden spoon.

Blind bake the cases for 90 seconds.

Spoon in the lemon curd and bake for 6 minutes.

MAKES 4 SMALL PIES

Hack it!

• Use store-bought lemon curd for a quicker tart, or try making lime tarts by replacing the lemon in the curd recipe with lime.

Lemon Pie

⅓ cup (80ml) lemon juice

¼ cup (25g) lemon zest

⅓ cup (70g) sugar

3 eggs

¼ cup (60ml) thickened cream

1 sheet shortcrust pastry

Place the juice, zest, sugar, eggs and cream in a pan and cook over a low heat for 10 minutes, or until thick.

Using a sharp knife or the cutter provided, create a circle from the sheet of shortcrust pastry to fit the hole of a family pie maker.

Press the pastry into the pie hole using fingers or a wooden spoon.

Blind bake the case for 3 minutes.

Spoon in the lemon filling and bake for 6 more minutes.

Remove the pie from the pie maker and, after it has cooled to room temperature, place it in the fridge for 1-2 hours to allow the filling to fully set.

MAKES 1 FAMILY PIE

Pineapple Upside-Down Pancakes

25g butter, melted

⅔ cup (150ml) milk

1 egg

1½ tbsps sugar

¾ cup (100g) flour

1 tsp baking powder

4 canned pineapple slices (in juice)

Combine the butter, milk, egg, sugar, flour and baking powder and whisk until smooth.

Place a disc of pineapple in each hole.

Place the batter on top of the pineapple discs.

Close the lid and cook for 2-3 minutes, checking regularly.

Carefully remove with a rubber spatula and flip to serve.

MAKES 4

Hack it!

• *Use a vanilla cake mix but replace the milk with canned pineapple juice. Sprinkle brown sugar in the holes of the pie maker. Arrange pineapple pieces on top then spoon over the batter. Bake for 5 minutes.*

Easy Custard Tarts

½ cup (125ml) milk

1 cup (250ml) cream

2 eggs + 3 egg yolks

2 tsps vanilla

1 tsp nutmeg

⅓ cup (70g) sugar

1 sheet shortcrust pastry

Place the milk and cream in a pan and gently heat.

Whisk the eggs and yolks, vanilla, nutmeg and sugar in a mixing bowl. Gradually add in the milk and cream, stirring all the time, until the custard thickens.

Using a sharp knife or the cutter provided, create circles from the sheet of shortcrust pastry to fit the holes of the pie maker.

Press the pastry into the pie holes using fingers or a wooden spoon.

Pour the custard into the cases until they are three-quarters full.

Close the pie maker lid and cook the tarts for 6 minutes.

MAKES 4

Chai Spiced Apple Pies

4 cups (480g) apple, cubed

1 cup (250ml) water

½ cup (110g) sugar

⅓ cup (115g) honey

1 tsp cinnamon

1 tsp cardamom

½ tsp nutmeg

1 tsp ground ginger

1 tsp vanilla

⅓ cup (50g) cornflour

2 sheets shortcrust pastry

Place the apple, water, sugar, honey, spices, vanilla and cornflour in a pan over a medium heat.

Heat until softened and syrupy.

Using a sharp knife or the cutter provided, create eight circles from the sheets of shortcrust pastry to fit the holes of the pie maker (note the circles for the bases should be larger than those for the tops).

Press the pastry bases into the pie holes using fingers or a wooden spoon.

Fill the cases with the apple mixture.

Place the pastry lids on top and close the pie maker lid.

Cook for 6 minutes.

MAKES 4 SMALL PIES

Easy Vanilla and Lemon Pie

1 x 400g can condensed milk

2 tsps vanilla

2 lemons, juiced

1 sheet shortcrust pastry

Place the condensed milk, vanilla and lemon juice in a bowl and mix thoroughly.

Refrigerate the mixture for 1 hour.

Using a sharp knife or the cutter provided, create a circle from the sheet of shortcrust pastry to fit the hole of a family pie maker.

Press the pastry into the pie hole using fingers or a wooden spoon.

Pour the chilled filling into the case until it is three-quarters full.

Close the lid and cook for 6 minutes.

MAKES 1 FAMILY PIE

Classic Apple Pie

6 cups (720g) apple, cubed

1 cup (250ml) water

½ cup (110g) sugar

⅓ cup (115g) honey

1 tsp cinnamon

⅓ cup (50g) cornflour

2 sheets shortcrust pastry

1 tbsp icing sugar, to serve

Place the apple, water, sugar, honey, cinnamon and cornflour in a pan over a medium heat.

Heat until softened and syrupy.

Using a sharp knife or the cutter provided, create two circles from the sheets of shortcrust pastry to fit a family pie maker.

Press the larger pastry circle into the pie hole using fingers or a wooden spoon.

Fill the case with the apple mixture.

Place the pastry lid on top and close the pie maker lid.

Cook for 8 minutes.

Once removed from the pie maker and cooled, sprinkle the pie with icing sugar.

MAKES 1 FAMILY PIE

Apple Custard Cake Pie

200g butter

1 cup (220g) caster sugar

2 tsps vanilla essence

3 eggs

1¾ cups (215g) plain flour

¾ cup (150g) custard powder

2 tsps bicarbonate of soda

350ml pre-made custard (such as Paul's)

1 x 385g can pie fruit apple slices

Make the cake batter by beating together the butter, sugar and vanilla essence in an electric mixer. Add the eggs and flour and gently combine.

Pour half of the cake batter into the family pie maker, then add the apples. Pour over the custard and finish with the remaining batter.

Close the lid and cook for 10 minutes.

MAKES 1 FAMILY PIE

Giant Banana Pancake

25g butter, melted

⅔ cup (150ml) milk

1 egg

1½ tbsps caster sugar

¾ cup (100g) flour

1 tsp baking powder

1½ bananas, chopped

2 tsps brown sugar

Combine the butter, milk, egg, sugar, flour and baking powder and whisk until smooth.

Pour the batter into a family pie maker.

Place the chopped banana on top and sprinkle with brown sugar.

Close the lid and cook for 3-4 minutes.

MAKES 1

Hack it!

• Save time by buying ready-made pancake mix from the shop.

Strawberry Tarts

½ cup (160g) strawberry jam

⅓ cup (70g) caster sugar

¼ cup (60ml) water

1 batch sweet shortcrust pastry (see recipe page 14)

¾ cup (200ml) pre-made custard (such as Paul's)

2 punnets strawberries

Mint leaves, to garnish

Place the jam, sugar and water in a small saucepan and bring to a boil. Reduce heat to low and simmer for 10 minutes until the sugar is dissolved and thickened into a syrup. Remove from heat and set aside.

Roll out the pastry to the desired thickness on a lightly floured workbench and use the smaller side of the pie cutter to cut out eight rounds.

Press the rounds into the pie maker holes to make shallow cases.

Close the lid and blind bake the tart cases for 8 minutes until slightly browned.

Place a tablespoon of custard in each tart case. Close the lid and cook for 5 minutes.

Top with strawberries and drizzle the syrup over the top.

Serve warm or cold, garnished with mint leaves.

MAKES 8

Hack it!

• You can use dessertspoons of strawberry jam for topping if real strawberries are not available.

Vegan Chocolate Tarts

½ cup (120ml) coconut cream

1⅓ cups (200g) vegan chocolate chips

2 tbsps coconut oil

140g vegan sandwich biscuits (such as Oreos), crushed

¼ cup (30g) almonds, crushed

60g vegetable oil butter

1 tbsp crushed pistachios, to serve

Heat the coconut cream in a pan until it begins to simmer.

Place the chocolate and oil into a heatproof bowl.

Pour the hot coconut cream over the chocolate and oil.

Stir the mixture until the chocolate has fully melted.

Combine the crushed biscuits, almonds and butter in a separate bowl.

Spoon the biscuit mixture into the pie holes, pressing it into the bottom and up the sides.

Fill the bases with the chocolate mixture.

Close the pie maker lid and cook for 4-5 minutes until the mixture has begun to set.

Remove from the pie maker and sprinkle with pistachios.

Place the tarts in the refrigerator for 1 hour to firm.

MAKES 4

Chocolate Lava Cakes

⅓ cup (40g) self-raising flour

1 tbsp cocoa powder

2 tbsps brown sugar

1 egg

2 tbsps milk

1 tbsp butter, melted

½ tsp vanilla

8 squares high-quality dark chocolate

Combine the flour and cocoa powder in a mixing bowl. Add the sugar and stir through.

In a separate mixing bowl, beat together the egg, milk, butter and vanilla.

Pour the wet ingredients into the bowl with the dry ingredients and stir until just combined.

Pour the batter into the holes of the pie maker. Push two squares of chocolate into the batter in each hole.

Cook for 6 minutes.

MAKES 4

Mini Chocolate Cheesecakes

80g plain or dark chocolate digestive biscuits, crushed

40g butter, melted

1 tbsp cornflour

3 tbsps sugar

250g cream cheese

1 egg

2 tbsps thickened cream

¼ cup (30g) cocoa powder

50g chocolate, melted

1 cup (150g) assorted berries, to serve

Combine the digestive crumbs and butter in a mixing bowl until crumbs are well coated with the butter.

In a separate bowl, whisk together the cornflour, sugar and cream cheese.

Gradually add the egg, cream, cocoa powder and chocolate, whisking the whole time.

Press around 3 teaspoons of biscuit base in each hole.

Place 2-3 tablespoons of cheesecake mix on top of each base.

Close the pie maker lid and bake for 10 minutes.

Once cool and removed from the pie maker, garnish with the berries.

MAKES 4

Index

First Published in 2020 by Herron Book Distributors Pty Ltd
14 Manton St
Morningside
QLD 4170
www.herronbooks.com

Custom book production by Captain Honey Pty Ltd
12 Station St
Bangalow
NSW 2479
www.captainhoney.com.au

Cataloguing-in-Publication. A catalogue record for this book is available from the National Library of Australia

ISBN 978-0-947163-66-2

All images used under license from Shutterstock.com
Printed and bound in China

5 4 3 2 1   20 21 22 23 24

NOTES FOR THE READER

All reasonable efforts have been made to ensure the accuracy of the content in this book. Information in this book is not intended as a substitute for medical advice. The author and publisher cannot and do not accept any legal duty of care or responsibility in relation to the content in this book, and disclaim any liabilities relating to its use.

ANTONIO MANZINI
TUTTI I PARTICOLARI IN CRONACA

MONDADORI

© 2024 Mondadori Libri S.p.A., Milano

I edizione Il Giallo Mondadori gennaio 2024

ISBN 978-88-04-77566-9

▲ mondadori.it

TUTTI I PARTICOLARI IN CRONACA

A Juan Carlos Onetti

Il segreto deve essere cercato non esclusivamente nell'intreccio, ma nel narratore.

ERICH AUERBACH